ENGLISH
FOR KOREANS

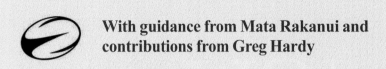

With guidance from Mata Rakanui and contributions from Greg Hardy

1 Are you crazy?

Intro

Ask these questions to your teacher:

- Is your name Dong su/Min hee? What's your name?
- Are you Spanish? Where are you from?
- Do you live in Gangnam? Where do you live?
- Are there 7 people in your family? How many people are there in your family?
- Did you study (major in) marine biology? What was your major?
- Do you often play badminton? What are your hobbies?
- Do you love eating kimchi jjigae (김치찌개)? What's your favorite food?
- Have you traveled to The Philippines? Where have you traveled?

Now ask these questions to your partner and ask follow-up questions ('Wh' Qs)

Warm-Up

What are Yes/No Questions? When do we ask Yes/No questions? Name as many Yes/No Qs as possible

- ▷ We ask **Yes/No questions** to determine a simple **positive or negative response**

- ▷ **Are you…/Is it…/Do we…/Does she…/Aren't we…/Isn't she…/Don't you…/Was he…/Were they…/Did I…?** are common Yes/No questions

Elicit an interesting example for each of the common Yes/No Qs above and write them on the board

1 _____

2 _____

3 _____

4 _____

5 _____

6 _____

7 _____

8 _____

9 _____

10 _____

Now students can open their textbooks and write correct examples from the board in the section above. Then take turns asking and answering these questions with a partner (ask more follow-up questions)

Are you Korean? No, I'm not.
한국사람이에요? 아니요, 한국사람이 아니에요.

Do you like watching movies? Yes, I do
영화보는 걸 좋아하나요 ? 네, 좋아해요.

Is your teacher good at singing? Yes, she is.
당신의 선생님이 노래를 잘하나요 ? 네, 잘해요.

Does orange juice make people healthy? No, it doesn't.
오렌지쥬스는 사람들을 건강하게 만드나요? 아니요, 그렇지 않아요.

Don't you like pizza? (You don't like pizza?) Yes, I do (like pizza). / No, I don't (like pizza).
피자를 좋아하지 않아요? (피자를 좋아하지 않지요?) 네, (피자를) 좋아해요. / 아니요, (피자를) 좋아하지 않아요.

Were you excited about coming to class today? Yes, I was.
오늘 수업에 오고 싶었어요? 네. 오고 싶었어요.

Did you take a bus this morning? No, I didn't.
아침에 버스를 타고 왔어요? 아니요, 안 타고 왔어요.

Make 3 other Yes/No questions with a partner

1 _____

2 _____

3 _____

Now change partners and ask these questions and discuss together (ask more follow~up questions)

Complete these sentences with a partner. Work together (while speaking out loud)

1 _____ **you busy** these days? Why?

2 _____ **your friends like to drink** makkeoli (막걸리) on rainy days?

3 You **don't want to** go out tonight? _____ **, I do / No, I** _____

4 _____ **your friend want to** join us for dinner?

5 _____ **you good at** playing pool (pocketball)?

Now ask these completed questions to your partner and discuss

Natural English

Practise the natural English expressions below

How are you? / How's it going? / How (are) ya goin'/doin'?
Good, thanks / Not bad / Pretty good

What's up? US/Canada
Not much / Just the usual

(Are you) alright? UK
(I'm) alright

G'day, mate Aus & NZ
G'day

Useful Vocabulary

Try to use all of these words in your discussions today. Check them off as you use each one.

Outstanding	뛰어난	Ridiculous	말도 안되는
Annoying	짜증스러운	Wonderful	훌륭한
Grow up	성장하다	Adorable	사랑스러운
Perfect combination	완벽한 조화	Unlimited	무제한
Classmates	급우	Leisure time	여가시간

Main Activity

Practise speaking using these questions using the correct grammar (verb tense)

> Ask more follow-up questions (Who/When/Where/Why/What/Which/How...?)

Are/Is/Do/Does...

Aren't you in a good mood today? Why/Why not?

Did you eat ramyeon every week in High School? Where? With whom?

Does your mother sometimes drink soju? How often/much?

Was there a TV show that you absolutely loved last year? Which one? Why?

Do your neighbors sometimes make a lot of noise? How do you feel about that?

Add 3 relevant and/or common errors from the students' discussion. Correct together on the board

1 _____

2 _____

3 _____

Please correct these sentences with a partner then check together as a class.

1 Is you confident when you speak in front of other people? _____

2 Are you boring when you watch romantic movies? _____

3 Were you lose your weight? _____

4 Don't your best friend has arbeit? _____

Take turns asking and answering the corrected questions with a partner.

More Yes/No questions... (Be sure to ask follow-up questions, also.)

Do you have a pet? What kind?

Don't you love having chicken and beer together?

Were you born in Korea? Which city/town were you born in?

Aren't you Italian? Where are you from?

Did you enjoy your life when you were in Elementary School? Why/Why not?

Take turns asking and answering the corrected questions with a partner.

Add 3 more relevant and/or common errors from the students' discussion.
Correct together on the board

1 _____

2 _____

3 _____

Please correct these sentences with a partner then check together as a class.

5 Are you convenient when you play with your friends? _____

6 Did you cut your hair? _____

7 Is your home nearby to here? _____

8 Do you like a cat? _____

9. Do you know my mind? _____

Now ask the completed questions above to your partner and discuss.

1. Introduction: What is a discussion and why do we have them?

An academic discussion is an organized 'conversation' about a specific topic that all the participants have been studying. Taking part is such discussions is extremely beneficial to participants and allows them to gain a deeper understanding of a subject, to exchange, develop and even change ideas, to improve critical thinking ability, to develop speaking confidence and to improve all-round language skills.

Indirectly, discussions may also improve motivation and encourage democratic habits.

Academic discussions form a key part of many university courses, and may also be an important part of your assessment. The skills that you learn through these discussions are also easily transferable to many other areas, such as interviews, presentations and debates.

 Discuss/Debate these topics with your partner or group

Do you think your university life is the best time of your life?

Why/Why not?

Is studying hard the most important way to get a good job?

Why/Why not?

Review

What did we study today? Please provide three examples with correct responses.
Say these correct sentences together as a class.

Building an Effective Professional Presentation

 Brainstorming (Choosing a topic)

Have you given a presentation before? In English or Korean? If so, how many times?
How could you have improved them?

_____

_____

_____

If not, think of some presentations that you have seen? What were the impressive and/or
disappointing parts of them?

Good points

_____

_____

_____

_____

Bad points

_____

_____

_____

Brainstorm some interesting topics with your partner (the environment, health, culture, science, nature, technology). Workshop the main argument that you would like to make on this topic.

Topic _____

Main argument _____

_____

_____

_____

Preview

Please read through the materials for our next class together. Prepare any questions that
you may have and we can discuss them in the warm-up session during the next class.

2 What's going on?

Previous Class Review

What did we do in the previous lesson? (Yes/No questions)
Elicit examples from students of:

- questions & answers
- useful vocabulary

Write these up on the board and practice them together.

What natural expressions did we work on in the previous class? (How are you?). Ask students for some key examples (prompt/guide if necessary). Put them on the board and practice saying them correctly together.

Warm-Up

What are Wh-Questions? How many Wh-Question words that you can think of? Why and when do we ask Wh-Questions?

▷ **What, Where, When, Who, Why, Which, How (much/many/often etc)**

▷ We ask these questions **to find out more information** about something

Make an interesting question for each of the Wh-words (and how) above

1 _____

2 _____

3 _____

4 _____

5 _____

6 _____

7 _____

8 _____

9 _____

10 _____

Now students can open their textbooks and write correct examples from the board in the section above. Then take turns asking and answering these questions with a partner (ask more follow-up questions)

Things/actions What is the healthiest food?
사물/행동 건강에 가장 좋은 음식은 무엇인가요?

Places Where is the nearest bathroom?
장소 가장 가까운 목욕탕이 어디인가요?

Time When will you go home?
시간 언제 집에 갈 거예요?

People Who do you live with?
사람 누구와 함께 사세요?

Reasons Why are you studying English?
이유 당신은 왜 영어를 공부하세요?

Choices Which city in Korea do you think is the best?
이유 한국의 어떤 도시가 최고라고 생각하세요?

Condition/quality How good is the Korean soccer team?
조건/질 한국축구팀이 얼마나 잘하나요[어느 정도 하나요]?

Frequency How often do you go swimming?
빈도 얼마나 자주 수영하러 가나요?

Amount – uncountable How much does a BMW cost?
양/액수 – 셀 수 없는 명사 앞 BMW는 얼마인가요?

Number – countable How many bottles of soju can you drink?
수 – 셀 수 있는 명사 앞 소주를 몇 병이나 마실 수 있어요?

Make 3 other questions with a partner using Wh-Questions

1 _____

2 _____

3 _____

Ask these questions to your partner and give the correct response

Complete these sentences with a partner. Work together **while speaking out loud**

1 _____ **do you think** is the best genre of music?

2 _____ **in the world** would you love to visit?

3 _____ **does the cherry blossom season** start and finish in Korea?

4 _____ **is your favorite** movie star?

5 _____ **do parents stick** Korean candy (엿) out the front of High School's on their kid's University Entrance Exam (수능) day?

6 _____ **kind of seafood** do you enjoy the most?

7 _____ **are you feeling** today?

8 _____ **do you go** to a sauna (bathhouse)?

9 _____ **homework** do you usually do each day?

10 _____ **people** live in Daejeon?

Practise speaking using these completed questions with the correct grammar (verb tense)

Useful Vocabulary

Try to use all of these words in your discussions today. Check them off as you use each one.

Fascinating	매력적인	Good value	품질이 좋은
Thrilling	아주 신나는	Sensational	선풍적인
Hit the books	벼락치기 하다	Once a year	일년에 한번
Refreshing	신선한		

Main Activity

Ask as many follow-up questions as you can to your partner after they say each of these statements. Take turns.
See if you can make 10 different follow-up questions for each statement

I ate lunch yesterday	I traveled here today
I will do something tomorrow	I watch TV
I exercise	I saw my friend recently

Add 3 relevant and/or common errors from the students' discussion. Correct together on the board

1 _____

2 _____

3 _____

Please correct these sentences with a partner then check together as a class.

1 When do most of people have a free time? _____

2 What height would you like be? _____

3 How do you think about living in Korea? _____

4 I don't know what is the problem. Do you? _____

After correcting the questions, ask them to a partner. Take turns.

Pronunciation practice

Practise the natural English pronunciation of the highlighted words below

Light	Right	Collect	Correct
Berry	Belly		

I really like to arrive alive after a very long flight in the rain
The royal lawyer was really loyal to his rural rival

'Red lorry, yellow lorry'

Add 3 relevant and/or common errors from the students' discussion. Correct together on the board

1 _____

2 _____

3 _____

More discussion questions (Be sure to ask follow-up questions, also.)

Who do you think is the best dancer in this class?

Why do you think many people visit Korea these days?

How many times have you been to an amusement park?

...How much fun do you usually have when you go there?

Where are you gonna go after this class?

Which local restaurant would you recommend?

How often do you breathe fresh country air?

Ask students to provide examples from their discussions using the 'useful vocabulary'

Add 3 more relevant and/or common errors from the students' discussion.
Correct together

1 _____

2 _____

3 _____

2. How to prepare for a class discussion

Preparing for your discussion is probably the most important thing that you can do. Basically, the better your knowledge of the topic to be discussed, the better your chance of successfully contributing to the discussion. Make sure that you go to all your classes, and carefully read any material for the topic. Useful discussions depend on students who have read and thought about the assigned material. Always also try to note any ideas that you feel strongly about.

Next, if you don't understand some of the material or don't feel confident about your ideas, speak to your professor outside of class.

Additionally, you might even want to practice discussing course topics and materials informally outside class with a friend or in a small group.

Lastly, you have to be prepared to participate in the discussion. If you find it difficult, set yourself goals and aim to increase your contribution each class.

 Discuss/Debate these topics with your partner or group

How big is the generation gap in Korea these days? Explain

Who do you admire? Why?

Review

What did we study today? Please provide three examples with correct responses.
Say these correct sentences together as a class

Building an Effective Professional Presentation

2. Welcoming people & introducing yourself (Opening & Focus Statement)

▷ Having chosen your topic and main argument, today we will develop our welcoming and introductory statements.

Firstly, identify your audience and decide how you will present for them specifically.
Who will be listening to your presentation?

_____

_____

_____

_____

How familiar are you with your audience?

_____

_____

_____

▷ Choose the relevant style for each of the categories below and write your choices in the spaces provided:

Welcoming

- Good morning/afternoon/evening,
- Nice to see you again,
- Hello/Hi,

- ladies and gentlemen
- everyone
- guys

Thank you so much for coming here today / Great to see you again / How is everyone today?

_____

_____

_____

_____

Introduction

Let me introduce myself, I'm_____ from_____

For those of you who don't know me, I'm_____ from_____

As some/most of you know, I'm _____ from _____

As you all know, I'm _____ from _____

Topic

As you can see (on the handout/screen), today I'd like to talk about…

This presentation will focus on…

Today I'm going to tell you about…

Relevance

Hopefully, this will be useful to help you understand about/how to…

This presentation will help you to become more familiar with…

Let me introduce the important topic of _____ to you

Preview

Please read through the materials for our next class together. Prepare any questions that you may have and we can discuss them in the warm-up session during the next class

3 How often do you sing to yourself?

Chapter

Previous Class Review

What did we do in the previous lesson? (Wh-questions) Elicit examples from students:

- make questions using as many different Wh-words (and how) as possible
- answer these questions together
- use new vocab from the previous class

Write these up on the board and practice them together.

What pronunciation did we practice last time? ('l' and 'r' sounds). What are some good examples to practice? Say these out loud with a partner to show your perfect pronunciation

Warm-Up

What are frequency adverbs? Brainstorm some from most to least frequent (often).

- **How often**…? asks about the **frequency of activities**
- **Always/almost always/often/sometimes/occasionally/not often/rarely/never** are common frequency adverbs

> **Students should provide some real-world, personalized examples**

1 _____

2 _____

3 _____

> Now students can open their textbooks and write correct examples from the board in the section above. Then take turns asking and answering these questions with a partner (ask more follow-up questions)

How often do you have rice during dinner?
저녁 식사로 얼마나 밥을 먹어요?

I always have rice during dinner (100%)
저녁 식사로 항상 밥을 먹어요.

How often do you do your homework?
숙제를 얼마나 자주 하세요?

I almost always do my homework (95%)
숙제를 거의 항상 하는 편이에요.

How often do you play computer games?
얼마나 자주 컴퓨터 게임을 하세요?

I often play computer games (80%)
컴퓨터 게임을 자주 하는 편이에요.

How often do you tell the truth to your parents?
부모님께 얼마나 자주 사실대로 말씀드리나요?

I sometimes tell the truth to my parents (60%)
부모님께 때때로 사실대로 말씀드리는 편이에요

How often do you go dancing?
얼마 자주 춤을 추러 가세요?

I occasionally go dancing (40%)
춤을 추러 가끔씩 가는 편이에요.

How often do you ride a bike?
얼마나 자주 자전거를 타세요?

I don't often ride a bike (20%)
자전거를 자주 타지는 않아요.

How often do you study all night?
얼마나 자주 밤새워 공부하세요?

I rarely study all night (5%)
밤을 새워 공부하는 경우는 거의 없어요.

How often do you watch TV shows in English?
영어로 된 TV 프로그램을 얼마나 자주 보세요?

I never watch TV shows in English (0%)
영어로 된 TV 프로그램은 전혀 보지 않아요.

Ask the questions above with a partner and give your own answers

Make 3 other questions with a partner using 'How often…?'

1 _____

2 _____

3 _____

Ask these questions to your partner and give the correct response

Complete these sentences with a partner. Work together while speaking out loud

1 **How** _____ do you travel to another city/town?

2 **I** _____ check the daily news. How about you?

3 **How often** do you _____ drinking games?

Now ask these completed questions to your partner and discuss

Useful Vocabulary

Try to use all of these words in your discussions today. Check them off as you use each one.

Heartbroken	가슴이 찢어지는	Wide awake (not fast asleep)	깨어있는
Scrub	때를 밀다	Generous	후한
Regularly	정기적으로	Bargain (haggle)	흥정하는
Exhausted	기진맥진한	Grateful	감사하는
Athletic	몸이 탄탄한	Frustrating	짜증나게하는

Main Activity

Practise speaking using these questions using the correct grammar (verb tense)

Ask more follow-up questions (Who/When/Where/Why/What/Which/How...?)

How often...

do your relatives visit your house?

do you feel disappointed that your class has finished?

do you play sports?

do you go to a sauna (bathhouse)?

do you thank your mother/father for preparing food for you?

Add 3 relevant and/or common errors from the students' discussion. Correct together on the board

1 _____

2 _____

3 _____

Add 3 relevant and/or common errors from the students' discussion. Correct together on the board. Please correct these sentences with a partner then check together as a class

1   Do you sometimes sing a song to yourself?   _____

2   I rarely trip another country. Do you?   _____

3   Does you often go to home using public transport?   _____

> Now ask the completed questions above to your partner and discuss

Natural English

Practise the natural English expressions below

What are you **up to** (doing now)?	**Not much.** I'm just watching TV.
Whatcha up to (doing) tonight?	**I'm meeting** some friends for dinner.
What are **ya gonna** do this weekend?	**Dunno.** Maybe just **hang out** at home.
What did you **get up** to on the weekend?	**Just the usual. I took it** pretty **easy.**
What have you been **up to** recently?	**Same old.** Just studying/working.

> Ask these questions to your partner and discuss.

26

How often do you… (Be sure to ask follow-up questions, also.)

go shopping at a traditional local market?   give presents to your family/friends?

go hiking?   argue with your brother or sister?

sleep for longer than 8 hours?

Ask students to provide examples from their discussions using the 'useful vocabulary'

Add 3 more relevant and/or common errors from the students' discussion.
Correct together on the board

1 _____

2 _____

3 _____

Please correct these sentences with a partner then check together as a class

4 How often are you drunken and overeat? _____

5 How often does you blind date or group meeting? _____

6 How often do you trip to overseas? _____

7 How often do you ask to teacher question? _____

After correcting the sentences. Ask the questions to your partner and discuss

3. Giving opinions.

Get involved early. An easy way to participate is to add to the existing discussion. Start by making a small contribution like agreeing with someone or asking someone to expand on something that they have said. Remember as well that if you are reluctant to speak before the class, try to say something early in the discussion. The longer you wait, the harder it becomes. Also, if you wait too long, someone else may ask your question or make the comment you intended to make.

In time you will be able to work up to answering questions that you have prepared an answer to, then answering general questions put to the group and finally disagreeing with a point.

- I think (that)…
- I feel (that)…
- In my opinion…
- I would say (that)…
- From what I understand…

- I believe (that)…
- It is my view (that)…
- As far as I am concerned…
- For me…

Check off each of these expressions after you use them in today's discussion

Discuss/Debate these topics with your partner or group

How often should people eat meat? Why?

How often should we have national elections? Why?

Review

What did we study today? Please provide three examples with correct responses. Say these correct sentences together as a class

Building an Effective Professional Presentation

 3. Catching the audience's attention (Finding a hook)

Techniques to catch the audience's attention in the first few minutes

▷ **Rhetorical Question**

How much danger is the world in if we don't address climate change immediately?

_____

_____

▷ **Relevant Story**

A few years ago, I was talking with a leading climatologist who told me…

_____

_____

▷ **Interesting fact**

Did you know that the world is getting hotter at the highest rate in known history?

_____

_____

▷ **Problem to consider**

Imagine the world in 2050 with the oceans 50cms higher. What can we do to avoid that happening?

_____

_____

> Choose at least one of these methods to catch the audience's attention for your presentation

 # Preview

Please read through the materials for our next class together. Prepare any questions that you may have and we can discuss them in the warm-up session during the next class

4 What will you do on your vacation?

Chapter

Previous Class Review

What did we do in the previous lesson? (How often...?) Elicit examples from students of:

- Common questions
- Natural responses
- Relevant vocab

Write these up on the board and practice them together.

What natural expressions did we work on in the previous class? (What are you up to?). Ask students for some key examples (prompt/guide them if necessary). Put them on the board and practice saying them correctly together.

Warm-Up

When do we use 'will/won't', 'probably will/won't', 'might'? Give some examples

- ▷ Talking about **future actions** that are **not 100% definite**
- ▷ Used to show **predictions, intentions, assumptions (hopes), arrangements**

Students should provide some real-world, personalized examples

1 _____

2 _____

3 _____

Now students can open their textbooks and write correct examples from the board in the section above. Then take turns asking and answering these questions with a partner (ask more follow-up questions)

Predictions
예측
My friend will become a teacher when she's older.
제 친구는 자라서 선생님이 될 거예요.

Intentions
의도
I probably won't drink too much tonight.
오늘 저녁에 아마도 너무 많이 마시지는 않을 거야.

Assumptions/hopes
가정/희망
My boyfriend might buy me a present for my birthday.
남자친구가 내 생일에 선물을 사줄지도 몰라.

Conditions
조건
If it rains tomorrow, I won't play tennis.
내일 비가 오면 테니스를 안 칠 거야.

Arrangements
준비
I will meet my sister after class. (Definite - I'm going to meet...)
수업 후에 여동생을 만날 거야. (확정 – 만날 예정이야.)

Make 3 other questions with a partner using 'will'.

1 _____

2 _____

3 _____

Ask these questions to your partner and give the correct response

Complete these sentences with a partner. Work together while speaking out loud

1 How _____ **you celebrate** after you finish your exams?

2 _____ **will your family do** for the next Chuseok holidays?

3 **Will you** _____ a book today?

4 What **time will you probably** _____ home today?

5 **Will you** _____ dinner with your parents tonight?

6 Which team _____ **win** the next Soccer (Football) World Cup? _____ **might be** the star player?

Now ask these completed questions to your partner and discuss

Useful Vocabulary

Try to use all of these words in your discussions today. Check them off as you use each one.

Morning routine	아침 일과	Emigrate	이민가다
Bachelorette	독신 여성	Elective	선택과목
Entertainer	연예인	Stadium	경기장
Addicted to	–에 중독된	Integrate/assimilate	동화되다
Humid (muggy/sweaty/steamy)	습한	Space travel	우주여행

Main Activity

Practise speaking using these questions using the correct grammar (verb tense)

Ask more follow-up questions (Who/When/Where/Why/What/Which/How...?)

Will...

Do you think **you'll (you will) be living** in the same place in 2 years (from now)?

Will you watch a TV show or movie in English this week?

Do you think **you might be** famous one day?

Will you live in another country sometime in the future?

Which subjects **will you probably study** next semester?

Add 3 relevant and/or common errors from the students' discussion. Correct together on the board

1 _____

2 _____

3 _____

Please correct these sentences with a partner then check together as a class.

1 Will you meeting your friends tonight? _____

2 Will you probably graduate your university 3 months later? _____

3 When might you make a girlfriend/boyfriend? _____

4 Will you be go to the library after class? _____

Now ask the completed questions above to your partner and discuss

Pronunciation practice

Practise the natural English pronunciation of the highlighted words below

What's the hardest thing about the **English language?**

Where's the best place to buy a **cheese sandwich** around here?

In which **months** do you wear warm **clothes?**

Did you see the **strange message** on the **fridge** under the **bridge?**

> Now ask the completed questions above to your partner and discuss

More discussion questions (Be sure to ask follow-up questions, also.)

When **will you go** to watch a live sporting game?

What do you think the weather **will probably be like** tomorrow?

When **will you get married?**

Do you think humans **will ever live** on another planet?

When **might you** next **eat** kimbap?

> Ask students to provide examples from their discussions using the 'useful vocabulary'

Add 3 more relevant and/or common errors from the students' discussion. Correct together and leave the sentences on the board

1 _____

2 _____

3 _____

Please correct these sentences with a partner then check together as a class.

5 Do you think your friend will marry with his girlfriend? _____

6 Where will you probably play with your friends on the weekend? _____

7 Will you absent class tomorrow? _____

8 Where might you go to vacation next summer? _____

Now ask the completed questions above to your partner and discuss

4. Observing and listening:

Observing

When you are taking part in tutorial discussions, try to observe how other students participate. Watch how the other participants ask questions, how they disagree or support things being said, how they clarify things, how they give their own opinions and long and often they speak for.

> **"If we were supposed to talk more than we listen, we would have two tongues and one ear."**
> **Mark Twain**

Listening

Listening is an essential skill and an important element of any discussion. Indeed it can be said that listening is the key to all communication. Listening is not a passive activity, and competent listeners don't just hear what is being said, rather they think about it and actively process it.

- ● being attentive and focused
- ● listening with an open mind and evaluating what is said

Practise these skills affer in today's discussion

 Discuss/Debate these topics with your partner or group

What do you think **will** be the most influential new technologies in the future?

How **will** the world's different cultural identities be affected by increasing globalization?

Review

What did we study today? Please provide three examples with correct responses.
Say these correct sentences together as a class.

Building an Effective Professional Presentation

 4. Structuring & Organizing

> **Introducing structure**

I'll be focusing on 3 main points/questions/issues related to…

_____

_____

_____

_____

_____

_____

_____

_____

Firstly, we'll talk about…

_____

_____

_____

_____

_____

_____

_____

_____

_____

Second/Next/Then/After that, we'll examine…

_____

_____

_____

_____

_____

_____

Finally, we'll take at a look at…

_____

_____

_____

_____

_____

_____

▷ Outlining organization

Handouts

Does everyone have a copy of the handout?

We'll be looking at a number of PowerPoint slides with some relevant information…

I'll be handing out copies of the PowerPoint information at the end of the presentation.

_____

_____

_____

_____

_____

_____

_____

Timing

This presentation should go for about 10 minutes…

It should take about 20 minutes to cover today's material…

Questions

Feel free to ask questions during the presentation.

If you have any questions, please wait until the end.

Preview

Please read through the materials for our next class together. Prepare any questions that you may have and we can discuss them in the warm-up session during the next class.

5 Do you want to go home?

Previous Class Review

What did we do in the previous lesson? (will) Give examples of:

- Common questions
- Natural responses
- Relevant vocab

Write these up on the board and practice them together.

What pronunciation did we work on in the previous class? (English Language/months). Write some key examples on the board and practice saying them correctly together.

Warm-Up

When do we use 'want to'? Elicit the relevant grammar. When is it used?

▷ **'Want to'** is used to express **wish or desire**

Brainstorm some real-world, personalized examples from students (to be written on the board).

1 _____

2 _____

3 _____

Now students can open their textbooks and write correct examples from the board in the section above. Then take turns asking and answering these questions with a partner (ask more follow-up questions)

Language Focus

| Want + noun | What do you want? | I want some coffee. |
| want + 명사 | 무엇을 원하세요? | 커피를 좀 마시고 싶어요. |

| Want to + verb | What do you want to do? | I want to sleep. |
| want to + 동사 | 무엇을 하고 싶어요? | 자고 싶어요. |

| Want + person + verb | What do we want our teacher to do? |
| want + 사람 + 동사 | 선생님이 어떻게 했으면 좋겠어요. [어떻게 하기를 바라세요] ? |

We want our teacher to make us work hard / We don't want our teacher to let us go early.
선생님이 우리가 열심히 공부하게 해 주셨으면 좋겠어요. / 선생님이 우리를 일찍 가게 하지 않으셨으면 좋겠어요.

Make 3 other questions with a partner using the 'want to'.

1 _____

2 _____

3 _____

Take turns asking these questions to your partner and reply and discuss together.

Complete these sentences with a partner. Work together while speaking out loud

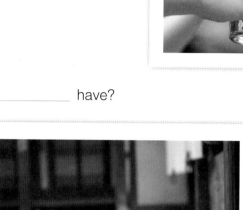

1 **Do** _____ **want** _____ **to** bring you some beer?

2 Where **do you want** _____ after class?

3 What **do you** _____ have for dinner?

4 What kind of husband/wife _____ **you want** _____ have?

> Now ask these completed questions
> to your partner and discuss

Natural expressions

Practise the natural English pronunciation of the highlighted words below

Do **ya wanna** speak more natural English? (Do you want to…?)

Whaddaya want? (What do you want?)

I want some coffee / **I wanna** coffee (I want a coffee)

Whaddaya wanna do? (What do you want to do?)

I wanna sleep (I want to sleep).

Whadda we want our teacher to do? (What do we want…)

We want…/We don't want…

Useful Vocabulary

Try to use all of these words in your discussions today. Check them off as you use each one.

A pushover	유혹에 약한사람	Courageous	용감한
Embarrassing	난처한	Hard-working	근면한
Bizarre	기이한/특이한	Unstoppable	막을 수 없는
Freezing/Boiling	꽁꽁추운/푹푹찌는	Coward	겁쟁이
A nightmare	악몽	Relentless	수구러들지 않는

Main Activity

Practise speaking using these questions.

Ask more follow-up questions (Who/When/Where/Why/What/Which/How…?)

Do you want/Do ya wanna…?

your parents to give you more money?

(to) never have to work again in your life?

(to) be famous?

(a) bunch of roses to be delivered to you right now? From whom?

(to) travel to every single country in the world? Why/Why not?

Add 3 relevant and/or common errors from the students' discussion. Correct together on the board

1 _____

2 _____

3 _____

Please correct these sentences with a partner then check together as a class.

1 Do you want live in the country? _____

2 Don't you want brother to remain single for his whole life? _____

3 Do want see alien life arrive on earth? _____

4 Do you want to play bowling this weekend? _____

Now ask the completed questions above to your partner and discuss

More discussion questions (Be sure to ask follow-up questions, also.)

Do **you want me to** stand up and act like a chicken?

I don't **want this class to** ever end. How about you?

Do **you want to**/(Do ya wanna) turn the air-con up or down?

Don't **you sometimes want to** tell your parents exactly what you think?

Do **you want to**/(Do ya wanna) be powerful?

Ask students to provide examples from their discussions using the 'useful vocabulary'

Write 3 more relevant and/or common errors from the students' discussion (on the board). Correct together.

1 _____

2 _____

3 _____

Please correct these sentences with a partner then check together as a class.

5 Do you want listening the music? _____

6 How many money do you want to make? _____

7 Do you want to climb the mountains after class? _____

8 Do you want to go to shopping later? _____

9 Do you wanna chicken? _____

Take turns asking and answering the corrected questions with a partner.

5. Some skills that will help you to become a better listener include:

○ Relax, focus on the speaker and clear your mind of distractions.

○ Help the speaker to feel at ease. Nod or use other gestures or words to encourage them to continue.

○ Maintain eye contact but don't stare – show you are listening and understanding what is being said.

○ Be an active listener and don't let your attention drift. Stay attentive and focus on what is being said.

○ Identify the main ideas being discussed.

○ Evaluate what is being said. Think about how it relates to the main idea/theme of the discussion.

○ Listen with an open mind and be receptive to new ideas and points of view.

○ Avoid prejudice and stay **impartial.**

○ Test your understanding; try to mentally **paraphrase** what is being said.

○ Wait and watch for non-verbal communication - gestures, facial expressions, and eye-movements can all be important.

> Check off these skills as you practice them during today's discussion

 Discuss/Debate these topics with your partner or group

Do you **want to** meet a world leader? Who would you choose to meet?
What questions would you ask them? Why?

Do you **want to** be in a popular movie? Why/Why not?

Review

What did we study today? Please provide three examples with correct responses.
Say these correct sentences together as a class.

Building an Effective Professional Presentation

5. Signposting & Transitioning (Paragraph 1)

You should now prepare your first main point for your presentation

_____

_____

_____

_____

_____

_____

_____

_____

_____

_____

Now you can outline your signposting and transition to the next section

▷ **Pointing out the end of a section**
This brings me to the end of my first point.

▷ **Summarizing each section**
Before we move on to the next point, just let me emphasize the main thing/s to remember on this first issue…

▷ **Transitioning to the next section**
Let's now take a look at / This brings me to / This leads me to the next point, which is…
Let's now examine the next point concerning/in connection with/regarding/related to…

 Preview

Please read through the materials for our next class together. Prepare any questions that you may have and we can discuss them in the warm-up session during the next class.

6 Mmm, this is tasty!

Previous Class Review

What did we do in the previous 5 units? Elicit 1 or 2 examples from each unit of:

- common questions, responses, vocab

Write these up on the board and practice them together.

What pronunciation and natural expressions did we work on in the previous 5 units? Ask students for a key example from each unit. Put them on the board and practice saying them correctly together.

Write these up on the board and practice them together.

Language Focus

Is it tasty? 맛있어요?	Delicious 아주 맛있어요.
Yeah, it's…/No, it's… 네, … / 아니요, …	Excellent / Great 정말 맛있어요.
How is it? 맛이 있어요[맛이 어때요]?	Good / Quite tasty 좋아요 / 꽤 맛있어요.

What does it taste like? It's…　어떤 맛이에요[무슨 맛이에요]?

Not bad / Pretty good 나쁘지 않아요[꽤 좋아요]/ 아주 좋아요.	Not great / Not so good 별로예요. / 별로 맛있지않아요.
Pretty bad / Terrible 정말 맛이 없어요. / 형편없어요[맛이 나빠요]	Disgusting 맛이 역겨워요[역겨운 맛이에요/토할 것 같아요]

Look at the pictures of food above. Ask your partner about the taste of each one and take turns answering – Do you think _____ is/are tasty?

Complete these sentences with a partner. Work together while speaking out loud

1 **How** _____ do you eat bibimbap?

2 **What** _____ you have for dinner tonight?

3 What **do you** _____ **to** drink when you eat chicken?

Now ask these completed questions to your partner and discuss

Useful Vocabulary

Try to use all of these words in your discussions today. Check them off as you use each one.

All-you-can-eat	양껏 먹을 수 있는	Starving	배고파 죽을 지경
Complimentary	무료의	Gourmet	미식가
Bloated	거북한	Pig out	선택하다
Fatty	지방이 많은	Once in a blue moon	아주 드물게
Nutritious	영양가가 높은	Hectic	빡빡한
A great cook	요리달인	Cafeteria	구내식당
Live by myself	혼자산다	Herbs and spices	허브와 향신료
Best in the universe	전 우주 최고의		

Main Activity

Practise asking and answering these questions using the correct grammar.

Ask more follow-up questions (Who/When/Where/Why/What/Which/How...?)

Where do you usually eat lunch?

Is samgyeopsal your favourite food?

Who do you think is the best cook in the world?

How often does your father cook?

Which restaurant do you really **want to** eat at?

Are you hungry now?

Add 3 relevant and/or common errors from the students' discussion. Correct together and leave the corrected sentences on the board.

1 _____

2 _____

3 _____

Please correct these sentences with a partner then check together as a class.

1 How many times have you overeaten when you were drunken? _____

2 How do you think about having pizza for breakfast? _____

3 Does one of your friends want to lose his weight? _____

4 How often do you have an appointment with your sister? _____

> Take turns asking and answering the corrected questions with a partner.

Natural expressions/Pronunciation Practice

Practise the natural English expressions and pronunciation below.

How are you? Not bad / Pretty good

Do you **really like** to **run** in the **light rain**?

What are you up to? Not much.

Have you ever dropped **a cheese sandwich** on your **clothes**?

Whaddaya gonna do this weekend? **Dunno.** Maybe just **hang out** at home.

More Discussion Questions

Practise the natural English expressions and pronunciation below.

How often do you get food delivered?

What's your favourite Korean/international food?

Which fast food do you think is the best/healthiest?

Will you eat out or at home tonight?

How much do you usually eat when you go to a buffet restaurant?

Do you think you'll skip breakfast tomorrow morning?

How often do you have junk food?

Do you usually want to have dessert after dinner?

Ask students to provide examples from their discussions using the 'useful vocabulary'

Write 3 more relevant and/or common errors from the students' discussion (on the board). Then correct them together.

1 _____

2 _____

3 _____

Please correct these sentences with a partner then check together as a class.

5 Will eating a lot of meat make kid's height bigger? _____

6 What do you want to eating when you are hungover (sukjae issoyo)? _____

7 When will you not eat during more than 12 hours? _____

8 Is there a McDonalds nearby to here? _____

9 What's your favorite menu at a Chinese restaurant? _____

Take turns asking and answering the corrected questions with a partner.

Presentation and/or Writing Topics

 Choose one of these topics and prepare a short presentation (with a partner/partners) and/or essay

- Is your life easy or difficult these days? Why?

- What do you think will be the biggest changes in the world in the next 15 years?

- How often do you think people should give money to charity? Why?

- What country do you really want to visit? Why?

- Why do you think so many people visit Korea these days?

 Preview

Please read through the materials for our next class. Prepare any questions that you may have and we can discuss them in the warm-up session during the next class.

7 What are you thinking about?

Chapter

Previous Class Review

What did we do in the previous lesson? (want to) Give examples of:

- Common questions
- Natural responses
- Relevant vocab

Write these up on the board and practice them together.

What pronunciation did we work on in the previous class? (Whaddaya wanna...?). Write some key examples on the board and practice saying them correctly together.

Warm-Up

When do we use the Present Continuous? Elicit the relevant grammar.

The Present Continuous is 'Subject + 'to be' + verb-ing'. It is used to describe:

- ▷ actions which are **happening at the moment of speaking**
- ▷ a **temporary event or situation**
- ▷ and emphasize a continuing series of **repeated actions** (with always, constantly, forever)
- ▷ **fixed plans** in the near future

Elicit some real-world, personalized examples from students (to be written on the board).

1 _____

2 _____

3 _____

Now students can open their textbooks and write correct examples from the board in the section above. Then take turns asking and answering these questions with a partner (ask more follow-up questions)

Language Focus

Happening now We are studying the Present Continuous.
지금 일어나는 일에 대해 우리는 현재 진행형을 배우고 있어요[배우고 있는 중이에요/배우는 중이에요].

Temporary Is it raining? Yes, it is. / No, it isn't. / No, it's not.
일시적인 일에 대해 비가 오고 있나요? 네. / 아니요.

Repeated actions My parents are always telling me to study harder/come home earlier.
반복적인 행동에 대해 부모님은 늘 저에게더 열심히 공부하라고/ 집에 일찍 오라고 말씀하세요.

Fixed future plans I'm meeting my friends tonight.
확실한 미래 계획에 대해 오늘 저녁에 친구를 만날 거예요.

Make 3 other questions with a partner using the 'present continuous'.

1 _____

2 _____

3 _____

Take turns asking these questions to your partner and reply and discuss together.

Complete these sentences with a partner. Work together while speaking out loud

1 What _____ **you doing** right now?

2 Who do you know that is _____ **complaining**?

3 What other subjects **are** _____ **studying** these days?

4 Where **are you** _____ immediately after class?

Now ask these completed questions to your partner and discuss

Useful Vocabulary

Try to use all of these words in your discussions today. Check them off as you use each one.

Downtime	휴식시간	High-maintenance	세심한
Tardy	늦은	Committed	열성적인
Slam dunk	덩크슛	Walking distance	도보거리
Kick back	쉬다	Cold snap	일시적 한파
Wandering around	거닐다	Blowing in the wind	바람에 날리는
Slim	날씬한		

Main Activity

Practise speaking using these questions using the correct grammar.

> Ask more follow-up questions (Who/When/Where/Why/What/Which/How…?)

What do you think Kim, Yu Na **is doing** at the moment?

Are you reading a book these days?

Who is constantly **coming** late to class?

How many people do you think **are sending** a Kakao Talk message right now?

Look out the window! **What's happening?**

Add 3 relevant and/or common errors from the students' discussion. Correct together on the board

1 _____

2 _____

3 _____

Please correct these sentences with a partner then check together as a class.

1 Do you working on an assignment at the moment? _____

2 Are you still work at your part-time job? _____

3 Why do you forever arguing at me? _____

4 What sort of music are teenagers listening to this days? _____

5 I'm thinking to contact G-Dragon. Should I? _____

> Now ask the completed questions above to your partner and discuss

Pronunciation Practice

Practise the natural English pronunciation of the highlighted words below

| They – Day | There – Dare | Those – Doze | Worthy – Wordy | Breathe - Breed |

Would **they bathe there** on **another day,** in **rather unworthy weather, though**?

Would you **rather** your **father** or **mother dare** the **other** to wear **leather**?

The question is **whether** to **bother** to **breathe** these **worthy words** or

whether you'd **rather doze.**

Do you want **this, that,** or **the other? Those** are your options.

More Discussion Questions

Be sure to ask follow-up questions, also.

Are you visiting your relatives this weekend?

Why **are** more and more people **becoming** vegetarians these days?

Are you going to a café this afternoon?

Is it snowing now?

Are you playing basketball with your friends after this class?

Ask students to provide examples from their discussions
using the 'useful vocabulary'

Write 3 more relevant and/or common errors from the students' discussion (on the board). Then correct them together.

1 _____

2 _____

3 _____

Please correct these sentences with a partner then check together as a class.

6 What are you wear? _____

7 These days, more people is using Facebook Messenger than phone texting? Do you agree?

_____

8 Do you think your English is improve? _____

9 Why do you always smiling? _____

10 What will you doing on the weekend? _____

Take turns asking and answering the corrected questions with a partner.

6. Asking for opinions

- What do you think?
- What's your opinion?
- How do you feel about it?
- Would you agree with that?
- Any comments?
- What are your views on…?
- How about you?
- Is there anything you'd like to add?

> Check off these questions after using them during today's discussion

 Discuss/Debate these topics with your partner or group

These days, more people **are getting** their news online.
What are the pros and cons of this?

Why is the climate **changing** so rapidly these days?

Review

What did we study today? Please provide three examples with correct responses.
Say these correct sentences together as a class.

Building an Effective Professional Presentation

 6. Emphasizing & Contrasting (Paragraph 2)

Here are some methods to emphasize certain points. Make some examples for your presentation

▷ **Directly identifying emphasis**

I'd like to stress/highlight/emphasize/point out…

_____

_____

_____

_____

_____

▷ **Rhetorical questions**

Just how worrying is this information? What do we do from here?

_____

_____

_____

_____

_____

_____

▷ **Strong statements**

What we need to do is…
This now becomes vitally important

_____

_____

_____

_____

_____

▷ Referring to previous sections

Let's go back to what I said earlier / As I previously mentioned,…

In addition to/Furthermore/As well as what we discussed earlier, let me also mention…

_____
_____
_____

▷ Contrasting

On the other hand/Conversely, some people argue that…, but…
Let's address/deal with/tackle the conflicting opinion that…

_____
_____
_____

Use any of these examples that are suitable and now prepare your second main point

_____
_____
_____
_____
_____
_____
_____
_____
_____
_____

Preview

Please read through the materials for our next class together. Prepare any questions that you may have and we can discuss them in the warm-up session during the next class.

8 What did you do last summer?

Chapter

Previous Class Review

What did we do in the previous lesson? (want to) Give examples of:

- Common questions
- Natural responses
- Relevant vocab

Write these up on the board and practice them together.

What pronunciation did we work on in the previous class? (they - day). Write some key examples on the board and practice saying them correctly together.

Practice these together with a partner for a few minutes.

Warm-Up

When do we use the Simple Past? Elicit the relevant grammar and write it on the board.

- ▷ The **Simple Past** is used to talk about a **completed action in a time before now.**

- ▷ The time of the action can be in the **recent past or the distant past** and the **action duration is not important**

Brainstorm some real-world, personalized examples from students (to be written on the board).

1 _____

2 _____

3 _____

Now students can open their textbooks and write correct examples from the board in the section above. Then take turns asking and answering these questions with a partner (ask more follow-up questions)

Language Focus

Regular I played the piano when I was in Elementary School.

규칙적인 저는 초등학교 다닐 때 피아노를 쳤어요.

Question Did you live in Seoul when you were young? Yes, I did. / No, I didn't.

의문 어렸을 때 서울에서 살았어요? 네, 살았어요. /아니요, 살지 않았어요.

Negative I didn't drink coffee this morning.

부정 오늘 아침에 커피를 마시지 않았어요.

Irregular I went home late last night. / I sat in front of my computer all day yesterday.

불규칙 어젯밤에 집에 늦게 들어 갔어요. / 어제 하루종일 컴퓨터 앞에 앉아 있었어요.

To be Were you shy when you were younger? Yes, I was. / No, I wasn't.

be 동사 어렸을 때 수줍음을 많이 탔어요? 네. / 아니요.

To be Was he in this class last month?

be 동사 지난달에 그남자가 이 수업을 들었어요?

Make 3 other questions with a partner using the Simple Past

1 _____

2 _____

3 _____

Take turns asking these questions to your partner and reply and discuss together.

Complete these sentences with a partner. Work together (while speaking out loud).

1 **My brother** _____ TV for 5 hours straight yesterday?

2 _____ **you buy** anything on the weekend?

3 **Did you** _____ how to swim when you were 10 years old?

4 _____ **you awake** at midnight last night?

Now ask these completed questions to your partner and discuss

Useful Vocabulary

Try to use all of these words in your discussions today. Check them off as you use each one.

French kiss	키스	Peck on the cheek	뺨에 가볍게 키스하다
Awesome	멋진	Stuffed my face	포식하다
Weekend trip	주말여행	Concentrate on	집중하다
Fried an egg	계란후라이 했다	Text messages	문자메세지
Model student	모범생	Stuffed	배부른
Lightning fast	번개같이 빠른	Impatient	참을성 없는

Main Activity

Practise speaking using these questions using the correct grammar.

Ask more follow-up questions (Who/When/Where/Why/What/Which/How...?)

Did you...?

eat breakfast this morning?

travel overseas last summer?

have a part-time job last year?

go to a nightclub (dance club) before you were 20?

cook something for yourself last week?

kiss someone yesterday?

Add 3 relevant and/or common errors from the students' discussion. Correct together and leave the corrected sentences on the board.

1 _____

2 _____

3 _____

Please correct these sentences with a partner then check together as a class

1 Did you looked at the subway timetable this morning? _____

2 What time did you came back to home last night? _____

3 Do you played Starcraft when you were young? _____

4 When's the last time you swimmed in the ocean? _____

5 Do you catch a cold? _____

Take turns asking and answering the corrected questions with a partner.

More Discussion Questions

Be sure to ask follow-up questions, also.

Was your dad a fast runner when he was young?

What movie **did you see** recently? Did you like it?

Did you have breakfast/lunch/dinner before class?

Who was the last person that **you called** (on your phone)?

How long **did you wait** for the subway/bus this morning? Or did you drive or walk here?

> Ask students to provide examples from their discussions using the 'useful vocabulary'

Write 3 more relevant and/or common errors from the students' discussion (on the board). Then correct them together.

1 _____

2 _____

3 _____

Please correct these sentences with a partner then check together as a class.

6 Did you ate jajangmyeon yesterday? _____

7 Was you drunken last night? _____

8 Did you overeat and your film was cut? _____

9 Do you play yoga in 2016? _____

10 What did you do on last weekend? _____

11 I met her two weeks before _____

Take turns asking and answering the corrected questions with a partner.

7. There are good ways and bad ways to ask other people for their ideas or opinions.

Good question types will encourage valuable answers, reveal information and stimulate conversation.
They include: open-ended questions that require longer more detailed answers (such as 'Tell me what you think about this?'); probing questions that require deep answers (such as 'How exactly did you feel on that day?'); hypothetical questions (such as 'What would you do if the university was suddenly closed?'); and devil's advocate type questions which are often challenging people's natural opinions (such as 'Pak Kun Hye shouldn't have been impeached, don't you agree?').
Bad question types are predictive or ask only for simple answers, which have a negative impact on the flow of a discussion.
They include: closed questions where the respondent has little chance to elaborate and need only provide a 'yes/no' type answer (such as 'Are you bad at taking exams?'). It needs to be noted though that these type of questions can sometimes be useful, such as to quickly check facts or confirm something; leading questions, which predict an answer (such as 'You are bad at taking math, aren't you?'; and negative or aggressive questions, which make a respondent less likely to want to answer.

Workshop some:

- ◯ Open-ended Qs
- ◯ Probing Qs
- ◯ Hypothetical Qs
- ◯ Devil's advocate Qs

together and write them up on the board.

Check off each of these styles of question after using them in today's discussion.

 Discuss/Debate these topics with your partner or group

Did you have a pet when you were growing up?
What attitudes and abilities did this help you develop?

Were you a good student in High School? Why/Why not?

Review

What did we study today? Please provide three examples with correct responses.
Say these correct sentences together as a class.

Building an Effective Professional Presentation

 7. Tools & Visual Aids (Paragraph 3)

▷ Here are some tips for using visual aids effectively

Prepare visual aids carefully and check them thoroughly for accuracy

Make sure they are easy to read (big enough/colorful)

Use clear and simple headlines on each slide

Follow the KISS principle - Keep it simple, (stupid)

Only use 5/6 bullet points per slide

Keep the text brief – maximum of about 7 or 8 words per line

Keep the information logical & easy to understand/follow

Let your audience know about the visuals – introduce & explain each slide

▷ Explaining

Let's take a look at this slide…

As you can see, the graph shows…

▷ Highlighting

I'd like to point out… and highlight the fact that…

You might be surprised to see that…

If you have a closer look at …, you'll see that…

▷ Looking at trends/graphs

As you can see,

the numbers have increased/risen/surged/doubled/dramatically increased/soared/skyrocketed

the numbers have decreased/fallen/dropped/halved/dramatically decreased/plunged/plummeted

Now prepare the third main point of your presentation and then prepare some visual aids to help your audience understand your information clearly

Natural Expressions

Practise the natural English expressions below.

See ya later.

Yeah, take it easy

Have a good one.

Thanks, you too.

Preview

Please read through the materials for our next class together. Prepare any questions that you may have and we can discuss them in the warm-up session during the next class.

9 Take it easy!

Relax And Take it Easy!

Previous Class Review

What did we do in the previous lesson? (Simple past) Elicit examples from students of:

- Common questions
- Natural responses
- Relevant vocab

Write these up on the board and practice them together.

What natural expressions did we work on in the previous class? (See ya later!). Ask students for some key examples (prompt/guide if necessary). Put them on the board and practice saying them correctly together.

Practice these together with a partner for a few minutes.

Warm-Up

When do we use 'Imperatives'? Brainstorm the relevant grammar and write it on the board.

▷ **'Imperatives'** are used to express **orders, instructions, directions, warnings, advice & requests**

Brainstorm real-world, personalized examples for each one from students (to be written on the board).

1 _____

2 _____

3 _____

4 _____

5 _____

6 _____

Now students can open their textbooks and write correct examples from the board in the section above. Then take turns asking and answering these questions with a partner (ask more follow-up questions)

Language Focus

| Orders | Get out! | Instructions | Open your books! |
| 명령 | 나가! | 지시 | 책을 펴세요! |

| Directions | Keep on going! | Warnings | Look out! / Be careful! |
| 지시 | 계속 가세요[계속 하세요]! | 주의 | 조심해! / 주의해! |

| Advice | Eat more fruit! / Don't smoke! | Requests | Help me, please! |
| 충고 | 과일을 더 많이 드세요! / 담배피지 마세요! | 요청 | 도와주세요! |

No smoking

Make 3 other questions with a partner using 'Imperatives'

1 _____

2 _____

3 _____

Take turns asking these questions to your partner and reply and discuss together.

Useful Vocabulary

Try to use all of these words in your discussions today. Check them off as you use each one.

Sit up straight	똑바로 앉다	Please be kind	친절해라
Turn around and go back	돌아가라	Don't lie	거짓말 하지 마라
Talk to me	나한테 말하다	Look me in the eye	나를 봐
Work with me	나와 일해	Hang in there	거기 기다리고 있어
Stop complaining	불평하지마	Never give up	포기하지마
Tell me something interesting	뭔가 재미있는 이야기 해줘	Shut up	조용히해

Imagine you are the military leader of your partner. Order them around for 1 minute. Now change roles.

You are now an extremely kind and wise life counsellor. Give good advice for a happy and healthy life. Take turns.

Now your partner is going to jog to your house. Give them directions (door to door). Switch.

Main Activity

Practise speaking using these questions using the correct grammar.

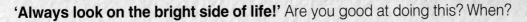

Ask more follow-up questions (Who/When/Where/Why/What/Which/How...?)

Just do it!

'**Always look on the bright side of life!**' Are you good at doing this? When?

'**Drink more alcohol!**' Is this good advice? Why/Why not?

'**Don't work too hard!**' Have your parents ever said this to you? How often?

'**Sit down and shut up!**' Who would you like to say this to? (except your teacher, of course)

'**Let's party!**' When you was the last time you heard this? Next time?

Add 3 relevant and/or common errors from the students' discussion. Correct together and leave the corrected sentences on the board.

1 _____

2 _____

3 _____

When giving instructions and directions, it's good to identify the order of actions:

First, go to a convenience store. **Then**, open a fridge and grab a beer. **Next**, pay for it. **After that**, go outside and find a comfortable place to sit down. **Finally**, drink it.

| Start a car | Buy perfume | Take a soccer penalty kick | Prepare cup ramyeon |

Take turns. Think of your own examples and ask your partner!

Pronunciation practice

Practise the natural English pronunciation of the highlighted words below.

Face	Pace	Fair	Pair	Firm	Perm
Fresher	Pressure	Fries	Prize	Faint	Paint
Fart	Part	Fashion	Passion	Four	Pour
Fork	Pork	Phrase	Praise	Laugh	lap
Referee (Ref)	Rep	Whiff	whip	Hof	Hop

Is it **fair** to **praise** the **phrase**, 'A **firm perm** shows a **passion** for **fashion**!'?

Are **four fries enough** of a **prize** if you **pour paint** on a **ref's face** and make him **faint**?

There's **pressure** to make the air **fresher** after a **whiff** of a **fart** makes you **laugh**.

More Discussion Questions

Be sure to ask follow-up questions, also.

'**Gimme** (Give me) **a break**!' When have you wanted to say this?

Where's a good café near here? Tell your partner how to get there.

What would you say to a young child who is about to cross a very busy road?

Everything your partner does makes you upset. Tell them. (**Don't look at me!/Stop holding your pen**! etc)

Recommend good things to do/not do if you travel to the U.S.?

> Ask students to provide examples from their discussions using the 'useful vocabulary'

Write 3 more relevant and/or common errors from the students' discussion (on the board). Then correct them together.

1 _____

2 _____

3 _____

Now, please also correct these sentences with a partner then check together as a class.

1 Eat medicine! _____

2 Drink more fastly! _____

3 Borrow me W10,000, please. _____

4 Listen your mother! _____

5 Don't teasing me! _____

6 Go to home! _____

7 Careful not do mistake. _____

8 Always do best! _____

9 See you again! _____

10 I dropped my phone into the toilet. What a stupid! _____

11 Frankly speaking, please write your sign on this print! _____

Take turns saying the corrected statements with a partner.

8. Agreeing

- Absolutely!
- I totally agree.
- I know exactly what you mean.
- That's a good point.
- That's true.
- I'm with you on that.
- I take your point.
- That's a great idea.
- I couldn't agree more.
- You're quite right.

> Practice these statements during today's discussion. Check them off affer you use each one.

Discuss/Debate these topics with your partner or group

Live your life to its fullest! (Seize the day! / Carpe diem!).

Why is this good/bad advice?

Be a better person! How can you achieve this?

Review

What did we study today? Please provide three examples with correct responses.
Say these correct sentences together as a class.

Building an Effective Professional Presentation

8. Summarizing (Conclusion)

As you can see, the graph shows…

Introduce your conclusion

Let me summarize/go over the main points that we have looked at today…

_____
_____
_____
_____
_____

Emphasize/Highlight one of your key points

Please remember the critical point about pressuring our politicians to bring about real change.

_____
_____
_____
_____
_____

Explain why this point is important

This is vitally important as changing personal habits may no longer be enough.

_____
_____
_____
_____
_____
_____

▶ **Refer back to your introduction & wrap up with a powerful statement/question/quote/directive**

As I mentioned, we must stop just talking and start taking action…

Let me finish by asking you a question, 'What do you think will happen if we all do nothing?'

As … once said, '…'

Now it's time for all of us to put this into action and I urge you to begin today.

_____

_____

_____

_____

_____

▶ **Thank your audience**

Thank you all for your attention. Much appreciated.

Now put together your own conclusion for your presentation

_____

_____

_____

_____

_____

_____

_____

_____

_____

Preview

Please read through the materials for our next class together. Prepare any questions that you may have and we can discuss them in the warm-up session during the next class.

10 What are you gonna do tonight?

Chapter

Previous Class Review

What did we do in the previous lesson? (Simple past) Elicit examples from students of:

- Common questions
- Natural responses
- Relevant vocab

Write these up on the board and practice them together.

What pronunciation practice did we work on in the previous class? (Imperatives). Ask students for some key examples. Put them on the board and practice saying them correctly together.

Practice these together with a partner for a few minutes.

Warm-Up

When do we use 'going to'? Elicit the relevant grammar and write it on the board.

'Going to' is used to describe:

▷ **intentions** (planned actions)

▷ **confident predictions** (based on evidence)

Brainstorm some real-world, personalized examples from students (to be written on the board).

1 _____

2 _____

3 _____

Now students can open their textbooks and write correct examples from the board in the section above. Then take turns asking and answering these questions with a partner (ask more follow-up questions)

FC서울 (Football Club Seoul)

Language Focus

Form
형태

to be + going to + infinitive

나 be going to + 동사원형 = ~할 것이다[~할 예정이다, ~하려고 하다]

Intentions
의도

I'm (not) going to meet my friend for coffee after class.

나는 수업 후에 커피 한잔 하러 친구를 만날 것이다[만날 예정이다, 만나려고 한다] / 만나지 않을 것이다[만나지 않을 예정이다]

Are you going to eat dak-galbi when you visit Chuncheon?

춘천에 가면 닭갈비를 먹을 거예요?

Confident predictions
확실한 추측(강한 추측)

That kid is (isn't) going to be a professional ballet dancer when he gets older.

저 아이는 자라서 전문 발레댄서가 될 것이다. / 되지 않을 것이다.

FC Seoul are 2 goals behind with 1 minute left. They're going to lose/They're not going to win.

FC Seoul은 (경기 시간) 1분이 남은 지금, 2점 뒤지고 있다. 그들은 경기에서 질 것이다. / 이기지 못할 것이다.

Make 3 other questions with a partner using 'going to'

1 _____

2 _____

3 _____

Take turns asking these questions to your partner and reply and discuss together.

Complete these sentences with a partner. Work together (while speaking out loud).

1 **Are you** _____ **to** play badminton this evening?

2 After I retire, **I'm going** _____ live in the countryside. How about you?

3 Are you **going to** _____ a hard time sleeping tonight after drinking 3 coffees?

4 I'm so tired. I think I'm **going to** _____ to bed early tonight. You?

Now ask these completed questions to your partner and discuss

Natural English

Practise the natural English expressions below

Whatcha gonna do tonight? (**What are you going to**…?)

I'm just gonna hang out at home. (I'm just going to…)

Where are ya gonna go after class? /

Where are ya going after class?　　(**Where are you going to go**…)

I'm gonna go da a café with a friend. (**I'm going to go to**…)

Get

When are **ya gonna get a taxi (take/catch) / present (receive) /job (obtain)**?

When does it **get (become)** dark these days? When **d'ya** think **ya gonna get (arrive/return)** home tonight? **Get (bring/grab)** your **stuff (things)!** Let's **get outta here (go/leave)!**

Make

You're **gonna make** mistakes, so don't worry about it!

Do **ya wanna make (earn)** a lot of money? Why?

Do

Are **ya gonna do** yoga/some exercise/your homework/some housework (chores) tonight?

> Brainstorm some other natural examples of 'get', 'make', and 'do' with your teacher and discuss.

Useful Vocabulary

Try to use all of these words in your discussions today. Check them off as you use each one.

Punctual	시간을 지키는	Go on a diet	다이어트 시작하다
Ludicrous	우스꽝스러운	Conscientious	성실한
Put my feet up	쉬다	Considerate	배려하는
Dye my hair	염색하다	Overcrowded	초만원
Let her know	알리다	Hair salon	미장원
Sharp	정확히	Pouring	퍼붓는

Main Activity

Practise asking and answering these questions using the correct grammar.

Ask more follow-up questions (Who/When/Where/Why/What/Which/How...?)

Are you going to study or relax tonight?

Why is/isn't your teacher gonna wear a pink dress tomorrow?

How are you going to be nicer to your parents as you get older?

Are you gonna work harder next class?

Where are you gonna go swimming when you go to Busan?

Add 3 relevant and/or common errors from the students' discussion. Correct together and leave the corrected sentences on the board.

1 _____

2 _____

3 _____

Please correct these sentences with a partner then check together as a class.

1 Are you going to cut your hair soon? _____

2 Who are/aren't you gonna go to dancing with (in Hongdae/Gangnam etc) this Friday night?

_____

3 Are you gonna review this lesson to home tonight? _____

4 Which famous restaurant you gonna go to this month? _____

5 Why are we gonna Dutch pay for dinner tonight? _____

Take turns asking and answering the corrected questions with a partner.

More Discussion Questions

Be sure to ask follow-up questions, also.

Are you ever gonna give up (eating) chocolate?

Where are you gonna get an ajumma perm when you're older?

When is your friend gonna meet you for lunch tomorrow?

Why are/aren't you gonna get a taxi home after drinking tomorrow night?

Or are you gonna stay out all night? When are you gonna call your Mom to tell her

you're not coming home?

> Ask students to provide examples from their discussions using the 'useful vocabulary'

Write 3 more relevant and/or common errors from the students' discussion (on the board).
Then correct them together.

1 _____

2 _____

3 _____

Please correct these sentences with a partner then check together as a class.

6 I'm gonna do straight home and sleep _____

7 Why are/aren't you gonna eat dog food at the start of next summer? _____

_____

8 Are you gonna study hardly next class? _____

9 Are you gonna have a wedding plan in the next 10 years? _____

Take turns asking and answering the corrected questions with a partner.

9. Disagreeing with someone and answering questions

There are a couple of important things to remember when you are disagreeing with someone in a discussion context. Sticking to them will ensure that the discussion continues to move smoothly and that unpleasant situations can be avoided.

The first of these things is to disagree politely. This can best be done by acknowledging the point or points that another person has made, and by staying calm and relaxed. It also goes without saying that if you maintain a respectful tone than the chances of someone listening and taking on what you have to say are much higher.

Secondly, you need to explain in full why you disagree with someone. If possible use facts and figures. Simply disagreeing with someone, without offering your reasons, is both impolite and unintellectual.

Disagreeing politely

- ▶ I know what you mean, but...
- ▶ Yes, but don't you think...?
- ▶ I can see your point, but...
- ▶ Well, I don't think it's as simple as that.
- ▶ I partly agree, but...
- ▶ Well, I'm not so sure about that.

- ▶ Yeah, but the problem is that...
- ▶ Yeah, that's true, but on the other hand...
- ▶ You could be right but I think that...
- ▶ I'm sorry to disagree with you, but...
- ▶ That's not entirely true.
- ▶ I don't think I completely agree.

Disagreeing more strongly

- ▶ I totally disagree!
- ▶ You must be joking/kidding!

- ▶ You can't be serious!
- ▶ No way! That's crazy!

> Check off each of these expressions after using them in today's discussion

Discuss/Debate these topics with your partner or group

How are you going to improve all of your English skills?

Are you going to travel overseas before getting a job? Why/Why not?

Review

What did we study today? Please provide three examples with correct responses. Say these correct sentences together as a class.

Building an Effective Professional Presentation

 9. Qs and As

▷ **Dealing with interruptions**

I'll actually cover that a bit later in the presentation.
Sorry, as I mentioned, let's leave the questions until the end.
If you don't mind, let's address that at the end of the presentation.

▷ **Introducing the Q and A session at the end of the presentation**

Ok, does anyone have any questions? Fire away!

▷ **Dealing with questions that are hard to understand or difficult**

I'm sorry. I didn't quite catch that. Could you please repeat that for me?
Sorry, I'm not quite sure about that. Maybe you could speak with ___ for more information.
I'm afraid that's not really my area of expertise. I will check on that and let you know later.

▷ **Asking polite questions**

Sorry, if you don't mind, I was wondering if you could please explain your point about…

Practice giving your presentation to a partner and asking them to ask you some questions. Take turns

 ## Preview

Please read through the materials for our next class. Prepare any questions that you may have and we can discuss them in the warm-up session during the next class.

II We're on vacation in 3 weeks

Chapter

Previous Class Review

What did we do in the previous lesson? (Going to) Elicit examples from students of:

- Common questions
- Natural responses
- Relevant vocab

Write these up on the board and practice them together.

What natural expressions did we work on in the previous class? (Whaddaya gonna do?). Ask students for some key examples (prompt/guide them if necessary). Put them on the board and practice saying them correctly together.

Practice these together with a partner for a few minutes.

Warm-Up

When do we use the prepositions of time 'in, on, at, during, after, later, for, by, until, within'? Brainstorm the relevant grammar and write in on the board.

▷ Prepositions of time: '**At**' is used to show a specific time, '**on**' is for a certain day, '**in**' describes a period of time. '**During**' is used before a noun of activity, '**after**' means when an activity/action has ended, '**later**' comes after a time expression that is not now, and '**for**' shows an intention of action in a stated time period. '**By**' means before a deadline, '**until**' describes an action continuing to an end point, '**Within**' means inside a limited time period. '**In**' also comes before a time period and means 'from now'.

Get some real-world, personalized examples for each one from students (to be written on the board).

1 _____

2 _____

3 _____

4 _____

5 _____

6 _____

7 _____

8 _____

9 _____

10 _____

In (from now): _____

Now students can open their textbooks and write correct examples from the board in the section above. Then take turns asking and answering these questions with a partner (ask more follow-up questions)

Language Focus

At 시간	See you **at 2pm** tomorrow. 내일 2시에 만나요.
On 요일, 날짜	I'm going back to Australia **on Tuesday / on July 7 / on Independence Day.** 화요일에/ 7월7일에/ 독립기념일에 호주를 돌아 갈 예정이에요.
In 월/년/계절	I'm gonna get a car **in December / in 2024 / in Winter.** 12월에 / 2024년에 / 겨울에 자동차를 살 예정이에요.

During	**During my vacation**, I wanna break up with my girl/boyfriend.
기간	휴가 동안에 여자친구/남자친구와 헤어지고 싶어요.
For	I'm gonna learn some Spanish **for my trip** in September.
목적	나는 9월에 가는 여행을 위해 스페인어를 좀 배울 예정이다.
After	What's the first thing you're gonna buy **after you get a job?**
-뒤에[-후에]	취직한 뒤 제일 먼저 무엇을 살 거예요[취직하면 제일 먼저 살 물건이 뭐예요]?
Later	Last year I lost my phone in Itaewon, but I found it **2 days later.**
-뒤에[-후에]	작년에 이태원에서 핸드폰을 잃어버렸는데, 이틀 후에 찾았다.
By (before)	We have to get fit **by the start of Summer!**
-까지는[-쯤에는]	우리는 여름이 시작될 때까지는 몸매를 가꿔야 한다[살을 빼야 한다].
Until	I will study for 10 hours every day **until our exams finish.**
-(때)까지	나는 시험이 끝날 때까지 매일 10시간 동안 공부할 것이다.
Within	If my brother doesn't get a job **within the next month,** my parents are gonna kill him.
-이내에/로[기간 내에]	만일 우리 형이 다음 달 이내로 직장을 구하지 못한다면, 우리 부모님은 형을 죽이려고 하실 것이다.

Take turns saying these examples to your partner and make some examples of your own for each one.

Complete these sentences with a partner. Work together (while speaking out loud).

1 Where are you **gonna go** _____ **class?**

2 I have to **finish my assignment** _____ 4pm _____ Monday.

3 I'm **going** to Seokcho **next Thursday**, but I'll **come back 3 days** _____ .

4 I'm really looking forward to **going to Guam** _____ **2 months.** How long will you stay there? I'll **stay there** _____ **5 days.**

5 I **have a yoga class** _____ **11am tomorrow** and I will **stay there** _____ **2pm.** _____ **the class** I will really do my best.

6 _____ **August** I'm going to China. I have to **prepare my visa** _____ **the next 6 weeks.**

> Now practice these examples with your partner and make some more if you can.

Useful Vocabulary

Try to use all of these words in your discussions today. Check them off as you use each one.

Drop by	잠시 들르다	Wander around	돌아다니다
My own apartment	내 소유 아파트	Play it by ear	되는데로
Dream partner	이상적인 파트너	Ancestral ceremony	제사
Free time	자유시간	Positive attitude	긍정적인 태도
Innovative	혁신적인	Efficiently	효율적으로
One-way trip	편도여행		

Main Activity

Practise asking and answering these questions using the correct grammar.

Ask more follow-up questions (Who/When/Where/Why/What/Which/How…?)

What are your immediate/short-term/long-term plans **after you graduate**?

You said you have another class **at 5pm**, but what are you up to **later**?

Do we have to prepare anything **for the next class**?

Where do you think you'll live **in 10 years**?

What do you think you'll be doing **at 11pm** this Friday night?

What do you usually do **on Friday nights in Summer?**

Now, please also correct these sentences with a partner then check together as a class.

1 I will go to my hometown 2 weeks later _____

2 We should complete our homework until p.m. 6 in Friday, right? _____

_____

3 Are you gonna stay at your brother's house during 2 weeks? _____

4 Do you have a flight to catch at Wednesday to 10pm _____

Take turns asking and answering the corrected questions with a partner.

Natural English

Practise the natural English expressions below

I'm gonna **meet my girl/boyfriend** in Sinchon at 7pm on Saturday.

I have **a doctor's appointment next Thursday** in Jongno.

I'm **going on a date** tonight with a girl/guy that I met the other day.

I have **a business meeting** to go to this afternoon at 3.

Sorry, I can't make the workshop on Sunday because I have **a prior engagement**. (Is it true?)

My friends and I are having **a get-together** on Friday night. D'ya wanna come along?

More Discussion Questions

Be sure to ask follow-up questions, also.

What do you think are the most important things to learn **during your time at university**?

Do you have to prepare anything **for Chuseok**?

What do you hope to achieve **by the end of this year**?

You will enjoy your life **until you get married**! Do you agree or disagree?

Do you plan to get married **within the next 8 years**?

Ask students to provide examples from their discussions using the 'useful vocabulary'

Write 3 relevant and/or common errors from the students' discussion (on the board) to be corrected.

1 _____

2 _____

3 _____

Now, please also correct these sentences with a partner then check together as a class.

5 Do you have a breakfast at the morning for the weekend? _____

6 Will you have a promise to play with your boy/girlfriend at 7pm on Friday? _____

7 Do you have a schedule to meet your seniors or juniors in the Summer vacation? _____

8 Would you like to marry with a talent after 5 years? _____

> Take turns asking and answering the corrected questions with a partner.

10. Summarizing the discussion

Evaluate what has been accomplished, assess what new learning people are taking home, and provide closure, e.g. through a summary of the main points, with the help of key terms or the day's agenda on the board, and by asking if there are questions, etc.

When giving a summary, we should cover all these points

- The problem in brief
- Majority point of view
- Dissenting viewpoints
- Whether the group has been able to reach a consensus or not

Check off each of these points when giving a summary of today's discussion

 Discuss/Debate these topics with your partner or group

Do you think smoking should be allowed in public **on** Friday and Saturday nights? When?

Do you think children should have a **curfew**?
What time should they be home **by**, and **until** what age?

 # Review

What did we study today? Please provide three examples with correct responses. Say these correct sentences together as a class.

Building an Effective Professional Presentation

Practice giving your presentation to a partner and asking them to ask you some questions. Take turns

 10. Using body language and voice effectively & overcoming nerves

▷ Discuss with a partner effective ways to use your voice and body language while giving a presentation.

Should you speak faster or slower than normal? What's a good tone of voice to use?

_____

_____

What kind of posture is professional and natural?

_____

_____

When is a good time to use gestures with your hands and arms?

_____

_____

Where's a comfortable place to keep your hands when not gesturing?

_____

_____

What's a natural way to make eye contact with the audience?

_____

_____

How can you emphasize important points using gestures and also your voice?

_____

_____

_____

Stressing words

How does the meaning of these sentences change depending on where you place the stress?

We all know that this is **extremely** important.

We **all** know that this is extremely important.

Using pauses

Where can we put pauses into this sentence to make it sound more impressive?

Now is the time that we must start changing our attitude.

Here are some tips to help you overcome your nerves

Be well prepared

Practice your presentation in front of your partner, friend etc as many times as possible until you are comfortable and, hopefully, confident.

Become familiar with the room and the equipment before your presentation

Arrive early and set up where you want to speak, prepare your visual aids, and make sure that the equipment works properly.

Be early and speak with the audience before starting the presentation

Get there before most people so you can set up comfortably and then greet people as they come in and talk to them before beginning your presentation.

Visualize yourself doing a good job

Picture yourself giving a brilliant presentation in front of thousands of people then this will be easy; or just imagine yourself doing a great job in this presentation and that should help with your confidence, also.

Try to relax

Do your best to breathe deeply and keep your muscles loose (not tense), especially your shoulders and neck.

Smile, be yourself, and try to have fun

If you are positive, natural and enjoy yourself then both you and the audience will feel much more relaxed and comfortable.

Focus on your information

If you know your material well and are enthusiastic about explaining it then you can concentrate on your message (and not your fears).

Turn your nervous energy into enthusiasm

It's ok to be nervous; almost everyone is. Try to use this energy to make your presentation more lively and interesting.

> Now give your presentation to a partner again while practicing using your body language and voice effectively. Take turns. Good luck!

Preview

Please read through the materials for our next class. Prepare any questions that you may have and we can discuss them in the warm-up session during the next class. Have a great day. See you next class!

12 Do ya wanna hang out on the weekend?

Chapter

Previous Class Review

What did we do in units 7 to 11? For each one, elicit examples from students of:

- Common questions
- Natural responses
- Relevant vocab

Write these up on the board and practice them together.

Practice these together with a partner for a few minutes.

Warm-Up

What are phrasal verbs? When do we use them? Elicit the relevant grammar and write it on the board.

▷ '**Phrasal verbs**' are very common in **natural, spoken English**

▷ The structure is '**verb + preposition**' or '**verb + adverb + preposition**'

▷ They are sometimes used to **show emphasis or completion**

▷ Much more often, they have a **totally different meaning** from the base verb

Get some real-world, personalized examples from students (to be written on the board).

1 _____

2 _____

3 _____

Now students can open their textbooks and write correct examples from the board in the section above. Then take turns asking and answering these questions with a partner (ask more follow-up questions)

Language Focus

| Verb + prepositionsition | Who will **look after** our baby while we go drinking? |
| 동사 + 전치사 | 우리가 술 마시러 간 동안 누가 우리 아기를 돌볼 것인가? |

| Verb + adverb + preposition | We need someone to **take care of** our kid immediately. |
| 동사 + 부사 + 전치사 | 우리 아이를 돌봐 줄 사람이 당장 필요하다. |

| Emphasis | When are you **stressed out**? Could you all please **stand up / sit down**? |
| 강조 | 언제 스트레스를 받아요? 여러분 모두 일어나 주시겠어요? / 앉아 주시겠어요? |

| Completion | C'mon, **drink up (eat up / finish off)**! It's time to go. |
| 완료, 종결 | 자, 다 마셔(다 먹어 / 다 끝내)! 갈 때가 됐어. |

| Different meanings | Please **put out** (extinguish) your cigarette. You're not allowed to smoke here. |
| 다양한 의미 | 담배 좀 꺼주세요. 여기서는 담배를 피우면 안 됩니다. |

Let's **put off** (postpone) our tennis match until next weekend. It's raining.

우리 테니스 시합을 다음 주말까지 미루자. 비 온다.

I can't **put up with** (tolerate) people who chew gum loudly in class.

나는 수업 시간에 소리 나게 껌 씹는 사람들을 참을 수가 없다.

Complete these sentences with a partner. Work together (while speaking out loud).

1 When you're **feeling** _____ , what do you do to **cheer yourself** _____ ?

2 Do you prefer to **stand** _____ in a crowd, or would you rather **blend** _____ ?

3 Who do you **take** _____ the most; your mom or your dad?

4 Do you think that capital punishment should be **done away** _____ ?

Now ask these completed questions to your partner and discuss.

Useful Vocabulary

Try to use all of these words in your discussions today. Check them off as you use each one.

Awkward	어색한	Luxurious	고급스러운
Reunion	동창회	Fancy	화려한
Hooked on	중독된	Stingy	구두쇠의
Essential	필수적인	Binge (drinking)	폭음하기
Kick back	쉬다	Get fit	건강해지다
Survive	살아남다	Pass out	술취하다
Black out	필름 끊기다		

Main Activity

Practise asking and answering these questions using the correct grammar.

Ask more follow-up questions (Who/When/Where/Why/What/Which/How...?)

Where is a great place to **kick back** on summer vacation?

Have you ever kept in touch with someone you've **broken up with**?

Do you usually have dinner at home or **eat out**?

How often do you **get together** with your high school friends?

Do you think more people exercise outdoors or **work out** at a gym?

Add 3 relevant and/or common errors from the students' discussion. Correct together and leave the corrected sentences on the board.

1 _____

2 _____

3 _____

Now, please also correct these sentences with a partner then check together as a class.

1 You look stressed! How can you endure that? Cheer up! _____

2 Come down! You can do it! Hang in there! Harden up! _____

3 How often do you going out with your friends? _____

4 What are some of your favorite places to hang up? _____

5 Does Hye-soo have a wedding plan two years after with her talent lover? _____

> Take turns asking and answering the corrected questions with a partner.

Natural expressions/Pronunciation Practice

Practise the natural English expressions and pronunciation of the highlighted words below.

There are **those that** wonder **whether they** would **rather doze, breathe** or **breed** in **this weather.**

See ya later! Yeah, take it easy! Thanks, you too.

After phoning your **friendly wife** on **Friday, feel free** to **half** or **fully finish filling** in **four** or **five difficult profile forms** in the **office,** if that's **fine, Phillip.**

Whaddaya gonna do after class?

Where are ya gonna **meet your boy/girlfriend** after your **appointment at the medical clinic**?

More Discussion Questions

Be sure to ask follow-up questions, also

How hard do you think it is to **give up** smoking?

What are some things that you couldn't **do without**?

What are you really **looking forward to** doing in the future?

Do you know anyone who's **blacked out** or **passed out** from drinking too much?

How would you **get by on** W10,000 for a whole week?

> Ask students to provide examples from their discussions using the 'useful vocabulary'

Write 3 more relevant and/or common errors from the students' discussion (on the board). Then correct them together.

1

2

3

Now, please also correct these sentences with a partner then check together as a class.

6 Have you ever fallen off with a friend or relative? _____

7 When you're worn up, what's a good pick-me-up? _____

8 What's a shocking surprise that you found away about a famous person? _____

9 Do you want to go to shopping later? _____

Take turns asking and answering the corrected questions with a partner.

Presentation and/or Writing Topics

 Choose one of these topics and prepare a short presentation (with a partner/partners) and/or essay

▷ What are you really **looking forward to** doing in the next few years?

▷ Where was the best place you **kicked back** last year?

▷ Give an example of a time someone said, **'Hang in there!'** to you.

▷ What are you **going to** achieve by the end of this year?

▷ What will you do **during** your vacation, starting in 2 weeks?

●● **ANSWERS**

●● **SAMPLE ANSWERS**

1 Are you crazy?

1. **Are** you busy these days? Why?
2. **Do** your friends like to drink makkeoli on rainy days?
3. You don't wanna go out tonight? **Yes**, I do / No, I **don't.**
4. **Does** your friend want to join us for dinner?
5. **Are** you are good at playing pool (pocketball)?

1. Are you confident when you speak in front of other people?
2. Are you bored when you watch romantic movies?
3. Did you lose weight?
4. Doesn't your best friend have a part-time job?
5. Are you comfortable when you play with your friends?
6. Did you get a haircut?
7. Is your home near here?
8. Do you like cats?
9. Do you know my opinion (what I think)?

2 What's going on?

1. **What do you think** is the best genre of music?
2. **Where in the world would** you love to visit?
3. **When does the cherry blossom season** start and finish in Korea?
4. **Who is your favorite** movie star?
5. **Why do parents stick** Korean candy (yeot) out the front of High School's on their kid's University Entrance Exam (Seunul) day?
6. **Which kind of seafood** do you enjoy the most?
7. **How are you feeling** today?
8. **How often do you go** to a sauna (bathhouse)?
9. **How much homework** do you usually do each day?
10. **How many people** live in Daejeon?

1. When do most people have free time?
2. How tall would you like to be?
3. What do you think (How do you feel) about living in Korea?
4. I don't know what the problem is. Do you?

3 How often do you sing to yourself?

1. **How often** do you travel to another city/town?
2. **I often c**heck the daily news. How about you?
3. **How often** do you **play** drinking games?

1. Do you sometimes sing to yourself?
2. I rarely travel to (take a trip to) another country. Do you?
3. Do you often go home using public transport?
4. How often are you drunk and throw up? / How often do you get drunk and throw up?
5. How often do you go on a blind date or have a group meeting?
6. How often do you travel (take a trip) overseas/abroad/ to another country?
7. How often do you ask a question to your teacher?

4 What will you do on your vacation?

1. How **will you celebrate** after you finish your exams?
2. **What will your family do** for the next Chuseok holidays?
3. **Will you read** a book today?
4. What **time will you probably go** home today?
5. **Will you have** dinner with your parents tonight?
6. Which team **will win** the next Soccer (Football) World Cup? **Who might be** the star player?

1. Will you meet (Are you meeting) your friends tonight?
2. Will you graduate from your university in 3 months?
3. When might you find a girlfriend/boyfriend?
4. Will you go to the library after class?
5. Do you think your friend will marry his girlfriend?
6. Where will you hang out with your friends on the weekend?
7. Will you be absent from class tomorrow?
8. Where might you go on vacation next summer?

5 Do you want to go home?

1. **Do you want me to** bring you some beer?
2. Where **do you want to go** after class?
3. What **do you want to** have for dinner?
4. What kind of husband/wife **do you want to** have?

1. Do you want to live in the country?
2. Don't you want your brother to remain single for his whole life?
3. Do you want to see alien life arrive on earth?
4. Do you want to go bowling this weekend?
5. Do you want to listen to music?
6. How much money do you want to make?

7. Do you want to climb a mountain (go hiking) after class?
8. Do you want to go shopping later?
9. Do you want some chicken?

1. How many times have you thrown up when you were drunk (drinking)?
2. What do you think (How do you feel) about having pizza for breakfast?
3. Does one of your friends want to lose weight?
4. How often do you get together with (meet) your sister?
5. Will eating a lot of meat make kids (get) taller?
6. What do you want to eat when you are hungover (suk-jae issoyo)?
7. When will you not eat for more than 12 hours?
8. Is there a McDonalds near here (nearby)?
9. What's your favorite dish at Chinese restaurants?

6 Mmm, this is tasty!

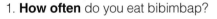

1. **How often** do you eat bibimbap?
2. **What will** you have for dinner tonight?
3. What **do you want to** drink when you eat chicken?

7 What are you thinking about?

1. What **are you doing** right now?
2. Who do you know that **is always complaining**?
3. What other subjects **are you studying** these days?
4. Where **are you doing** immediately after class?

1. Are you working on an assignment at the moment?
2. Are you still working at your part-time job?
3. Why are you forever arguing with me?
4. What sort of music are teenagers listening to these days?
5. I'm thinking about contacting G-Dragon. Should I?
6. What are you wearing?
7. These days, more people are using Facebook Messenger than texting? Do you agree?
8. Do you think your English is improving?
9. Why are you always smiling?
10. What will you be doing on the weekend?

1. Did you look at the subway timetable this morning?
2. What time did you come back home last night?
3. Did you play Starcraft when you were young?
4. When's the last time you swam in the ocean?
5. Did you catch a cold (Do you have a cold)?
6. Did you eat jajangmyeon yesterday?
7. Were you drunk last night?
8. Did you throw up and black out (lose your memory)?
9. Did you do yoga in 2016?
10. What did you do last weekend?
11. I met her two weeks ago

8   What did you do last summer?

1. **My brother watched** TV for 5 hours straight yesterday?
2. **Did you buy** anything on the weekend?
3. **Did you know** how to swim when you were 10 years old?
4. **Were you awake** at midnight last night?

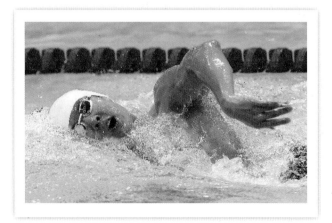

9 Take it easy!

1. Take medicine!
2. Drink faster (more quickly)!
3. Lend me (Let me borrow) W10,000, please.
4. Listen to your mother!
5. Don't tease me!
6. Go home!
7. Be careful not to make a mistake.
8. Always do your best!
9. See you next time!
10. I dropped my phone into the toilet. How stupid (am I)!
11. (To be honest), please sign here!

1. Are you going to get a haircut soon?
2. Who are/aren't you gonna go dancing with (in Hong-dae/Gangnam etc) this Friday night?
3. Are you gonna review this lesson at home tonight?
4. Which famous restaurant are you gonna go to this month?
5. Why are we gonna pay separately at dinner tonight?
6. I'm gonna go straight home and sleep
7. Why are/aren't you gonna eat dog food at the start of next summer?
8. Are you gonna study hard next class?
9. Are you gonna get married in the next 10 years?

10 What are you gonna do tonight?

1. **Are you going to** play badminton this evening?
2. After I retire, **I'm going to** live in the countryside. How about you?
3. Are you **going to have** a hard time sleeping tonight after drinking 3 coffees?
4. I'm so tired. I think I'm **going to go** to bed early to-night. You?

11 We're on vacation in 3 weeks

1. Where are you **gonna go after class**?
2. I have to **finish my assignment by 4pm on Monda**y.
3. I'm **going** to Seokcho **next Thursday**, but I'll **come back 3 days later**
4. I'm really looking forward to **going to Guam in 2 months.** How long will you stay there? I'll **stay there for 5 days.**
5. I **have a yoga class at 11am tomorrow** and I will **stay there until 2pm. After the class** I will really do my best.
6. **In August** I'm going to China. I have to **prepare my visa within the next 6 weeks.**

1. I will go to my hometown in 2 weeks
2. We should complete our homework by p.m. 6 on Friday, right?
3. I'm gonna stay at my brother's house for 2 weeks
4. I have a flight to catch on Wednesday at 10pm
5. Did you have breakfast in the morning on the weekend?
6. Do you plan to meet your boy/girlfriend at 7pm on Friday?
7. Do you plan to meet your friends in the Summer vacation?
8. Would you like to get married to a celebrity in 5 years?

12 Do ya wanna hang out on the weekend?

1. When you're **feeling down** what do you do to **cheer yourself up?**
2. Do you prefer to **stand out** in a crowd, or would you rather **blend in**?
3. Who do you **take after** the most; your mom or your dad?
4. Do you think that capital punishment should be **done away with?**

1. You look stressed! How can you put up with that? Don't give up!
2. Calm down! You can do it! Hang in there! Harden up!
3. How often do you go out with your friends?
4. What are some of your favorite places to hang out?
5. Does Hye-soo plan to get married in 2 years with her celebrity (famous) partner (fiancé)?
6. Have you ever fallen out with a friend or relative?
7. When you're worn out, what's a good pick-me-up?
8. What's a shocking surprise that you found out about a famous person?
9. Do you want to go shopping later?

1 **Are you crazy?**

Useful Vocabulary

Try to use all of these words in your discussions to-day. Check them off as you use each one.

Outstanding	뛰어난	Ridiculous	말도 안되는
Annoying	짜증스러운	Wonderful	훌륭한
Grow up	성장하다	Adorable	사랑스러운
Perfect combination	완벽한 조화	Unlimited	무제한
Classmates	급우	Leisure time	여가시간

Main Activity

Are/Is/Do/Does…

▷ **Aren't you** in a good mood today? Why/Why not?

▷ Actually, I'm in a **wonderful** mood today.

▷ **Did you** eat ramyeon every week in High School? Where? With whom?

▷ Yeah, even though it's not so healthy, my **classmates** and I often ate ramyeon in high school.

▷ **Does your** mother sometimes drink soju? How often/much?

▷ Yeah, my mom often drinks **unlimited** amounts of soju.

▷ **Was there** a TV show that you absolutely loved last year? Which one? Why?

▷ Yeah, I thought that last year's episodes of 'Black Mirror' were **outstanding** because…

▷ **Do your** neighbors sometimes make a lot of noise? How **do you** feel about that?

▷ Yes. I find it to be extremely **annoying** when my neighbors make a lot of noise.

More Yes/No questions…

(Be sure to ask follow-up questions, also.)

▷ **Do you have** a pet? What kind?

▷ Yes, I have an **adorable** puppy called Bruce.

▷ **Don't you** love having chicken and beer together?

▷ Yep, I love having chicken with beer. I think it's a **perfect combination.**

▷ **Were you** born in Korea? Which city/town were you born in?

▷ No, I was born in England and I **grew up** in Australia.

▷ **Aren't you** Italian? Where are you from?

▷ Please don't be **ridiculous.** You know that I'm from Korea.

▷ **Did you** enjoy your life when you were in Elementary School? Why/Why not?

▷ Yeah, I did because I had a lot of **leisure time** when I was young

2 What's going on?

Useful Vocabulary

 Try to use all of these words in your discussions to-day. Check them off as you use each one.

Fascinating	매력적인	Good value	품질이 좋은
Thrilling	아주 신나는	Sensational	선풍적인
Hit the books	벼락치기 하다	Once a year	일년에 한번
Refreshing	신선한		

More discussion questions
(Be sure to ask follow-up questions, also.)

- ▶ **Who** do you think is the best dancer in this class?
- ▶ Our teacher is a **sensational** dancer.

- ▶ **Why** do you think many people visit Korea these days?
- ▶ Many international people find Korea to be **fascinating**

- ▶ **How many** times have you been to an amusement park?
- ▶ Lots of times. I probably go about **once a year.**

- ▶ **...How much** fun do you usually have when you go there?
- ▶ I think they're **thrilling.**

- ▶ **Where** are you gonna go after this class?
- ▶ I'm probably gonna go home and **hit the books** as I have a test tomorrow.

- ▶ **Which** local restaurant would you recommend?
- ▶ There's a restaurant just around the corner that I think is really **good value.**

- ▶ **How often** do you breathe fresh country air?
- ▶ As often as possible. It's very **refreshing**

3 How often do you sing to yourself?

Useful Vocabulary

 Try to use all of these words in your discussions to-day. Check them off as you use each one.

Heartbroken	가슴이 찢어지는	Wide awake (not fast asleep)	깨어있는
Scrub	때를 밀다	Generous	후한
Regularly	정기적으로	Bargain (haggle)	흥정하는
Exhausted	기진맥진한	Grateful	감사하는
Athletic	몸이 탄탄한	Frustrating	짜증나게하는

How often...

- ▶ do your relatives visit your house?
- ▶ My relatives **regularly** visit my home.

- ▶ do you feel disappointed that your class has finished?
- ▶ Sure. I always feel **heartbroken** when this class finishes.

- do you play sports?
- Nah, not very often at all. I'm not very **athletic.**

- do you go to a sauna (bathhouse)?
- I occasionally go to a sauna to **scrub** myself perfectly clean.

- do you thank your mother/father for preparing food for you?
- I rarely thank my mom for preparing my meals even though I am **grateful**

How often do you...
(Be sure to ask follow-up questions, also.)

- go shopping at a traditional local market?
- I sometimes go shopping at a traditional market because I'm good at **bargaining (haggling).**

- give presents to your family/friends?
- I often give presents to my family and friends because I'm quite **generous.**

- go hiking?
- I don't often go hiking because I feel **exhausted** when I get to the top of a mountain.

- argue with your brother or sister?
- I almost always argue with my brother, which is very **frustrating.**

- sleep for longer than 8 hours?
- I rarely sleep for longer than 8 hours, as I'm often **wide awake** at 3am.

4 What will you do on your vacation?

Useful Vocabulary

Try to use all of these words in your discussions to-day. Check them off as you use each one.

Morning routine	아침 일과	Emigrate	이민가다
Bachelorette	독신 여성	Elective	선택과목
Entertainer	연예인	Stadium	경기장
Addicted to	–에 중독된	Integrate/ assimilate	동화되다
Humid (muggy/ sweaty/steamy)	습한	Space travel	우주여행

Main Activity
Practise speaking using these questions using the correct grammar (verb tense)

Ask more follow-up questions (Who/When/Where/Why/What/Which/How...?)

Will...

- Do you think **you'll (you will) be living** in the same place in 2 years (from now)?
- I'll probably be in the same place unless **I emigrate** to Canada.

- **Will you watch** a TV show or movie in English this week?
- Yeah, I'm **addicted to** English TV shows, like Sherlock.

- Do you think **you might be famous** one day?
- I hope so; I really wanna be an **entertainer**, hopefully a singer.

- **Will you live** in another country sometime in the future?
- I'd really like to live in New Zealand, where I hope to **integrate/ assimilate** into local society.

STAR

- Which subjects **will you probably study** next semester?
- I've finished most of my required subjects, so I will choose some **electives** next semester.

More discussion questions...
(Be sure to ask follow-up questions, also.)

- When **will you go** to watch a live sporting game?
- I plan to go out to the **stadium** to watch my baseball team soon.

- What do you think the weather **will probably be like** tomorrow?
- It'll probably be pretty **humid** again tomorrow.

- When **will you get married**?
- I don't wanna get married. I wanna be a bachelor/ **bachelorette** forever.

- Do you think humans **will ever live** on another planet?
- Maybe. With improvements in technology, **space travel** might become much easier in the future.

- When **might you** next **eat** kimbap?
- I'll maybe eat kimbap tomorrow, as it's often part of my **morning routine.**

5 Do you want to go home?

Useful Vocabulary

 Try to use all of these words in your discussions today. Check them off as you use each one.

Morning routine	아침 일과	Emigrate	이민가다
Bachelorette	독신 여성	Elective	선택과목
Entertainer	연예인	Stadium	경기장
Addicted to	–에 중독된	Integrate/ assimilate	동화되다
Humid (muggy/ sweaty/steamy)	습한	Space travel	우주여행

Main Activity
Practise speaking using these questions.

Ask more follow-up questions (Who/When/Where/Why/What/Which/How…?)

Do you want/Do ya wanna…?

- your parents to give you more money?
- Sure. My Dad's a **pushover**; he always gives me money when I ask him.

- (to) never have to work again in your life?
- No, I'd feel guilty. I'm naturally **hard-working.**

- (to) be famous?
- No, I would hate the **relentless** attention.

- (a) bunch of roses to be delivered to you right now? From whom?
- Sounds great, but it would be too **embarrassing** if they arrived during class.

- (to) travel to every single country in the world? Why/Why not?
- Maybe not. I'm not **courageous** enough to want to go everywhere.

More discussion questions...
(Be sure to ask follow-up questions, also.)

- **Do you want me to** stand up and act like a chicken?
- That sounds **bizarre**, but OK.

- **I don't want this class to** ever end. How about you?
- I do. A never-ending class sounds like **a nightmare.**

- **Do you want to**/(Do ya wanna) turn the air-con up or down?
- Yeah. Could we turn the air-con up/down? I'm **freezing/boiling.**

- **Don't you sometimes want to** tell your parents exactly what you think?
- Yeah, I do, but I'm too much of a **coward** to actually tell them.

- **Do you want to**/(Do ya wanna) be powerful?
- I'm already **unstoppable** when I do my best.

 Mmm, this is tasty!

Useful Vocabulary

 Try to use all of these words in your discussions today. Check them off as you use each one.

All-you-can-eat	양껏 먹을 수 있는	Starving	배고파 죽을 지경
Complimentary	무료의	Gourmet	미식가
Bloated	거북한	Pig out	선택하다
Fatty	지방이 많은	Once in a blue moon	아주 드물게
Nutritious	영양가가 높은	Hectic	빡빡한
A great cook	요리달인	Cafeteria	구내식당
Live by myself	혼자산다	Herbs and spices	허브와 향신료
Best in the universe	전 우주 최고의		

Main Activity
Practise asking and answering these questions using the correct grammar.

Ask more follow-up questions
(Who/When/Where/Why/What/Which/How…?)

- **Where** do you usually eat lunch?
- I usually go to the nearby school **cafeteria**; it's cheap and the food is not too bad.

- **Is** samgyeopsal your favourite food?
- Maybe not; it's tasty, but a bit too **fatty** for me.

- **Who** do you think is the best cook in the world?
- My mom is not only the best cook in the world, but also the **best in the universe.**

- **How often** does your father cook?
- My father cooks **once in a blue moon.**

- Which restaurant do you really **want to** eat at?
- I really wanna eat at a **gourmet** restaurant in Paris.

- **Are** you hungry now?
- Yeah, I'm absolutely **starving.**

More discussion questions...
(Be sure to ask follow-up questions, also.)

- **How often** do you get food delivered?
- **I live by myself**, so I get food delivered almost every day.

- **What's** your favourite Korean/international food?
- I absolutely love Thai food. I particularly like the unique **herbs and spices**.

- **Which** fast food do you think is the best/healthiest?
- I think maybe kimbap is the most **nutritious** fast food.

- **Will** you eat out or at home tonight?
- I'll probably eat at home, as my mom is **a great cook**.

- **How much** do you usually eat when you go to a buffet restaurant?
- I always **pig out** when I go to an **all-you-can-eat** restaurant.

- Do you think **you'll** skip breakfast tomorrow morning?
- Yeah, probably. I have a **hectic** morning routine.

- **How often** do you have junk food?
- I try to avoid junk food, as it always makes me feel **bloated.**

- Do you usually **want to** have dessert after dinner?
- I usually skip dessert, unless it's **complimentary.**

7 What are you thinking about?

Useful Vocabulary

 Try to use all of these words in your discussions today. Check them off as you use each one

Downtime	휴식시간	High-maintenance	세심한
Tardy	늦은	Committed	열성적인
Slam dunk	덩크슛	Walking distance	도보거리
Kick back	쉬다	Cold snap	일시적 한파
Wandering around	거닐다	Blowing in the wind	바람에 날리는
Slim	날씬한		

Main Activity

Practise speaking using these questions using the correct grammar.

Ask more follow-up questions (Who/When/Where/Why/What/Which/How...?)

▷ What do you think Kim, Yu Na **is doing** at the moment?

▷ Hopefully she's enjoying some well-deserved **downtime.**

▷ **Are you reading** a book these days?

▷ Yeah, I am. I'm a fairly **committed** reader.

▷ Who **is** constantly **coming** late to class?

▷ Actually, my partner is consistently a little bit **tardy.**

▷ How many people do you think **are sending** a Kakao Talk message right now?

▷ My girlfriend is probably sending me a message right now, as she's very **high-maintenance**.

▷ Look out the window! **What's happening**?

▷ People are **wandering around** and leaves are **blowing in the wind**.

More discussion questions...

(Be sure to ask follow-up questions, also.)

▷ **Are you visiting** your relatives this weekend?

▷ Unfortunately, yes. They live **walking distance** from our place.

▷ Why **are** more and more people **becoming** vegetarians these days?

▷ Possibly because they want to be **slim**, or maybe because of animal rights or environmental reasons.

▷ **Are you going** to a café this afternoon?

▷ Yeah, I think I might. I feel like **kicking back** with my friends.

▷ **Is it snowing** now?

▷ Yeah, it is. We're in the middle of a **cold snap**.

▷ **Are you playing** basketball with your friends after this class?

▷ Actually, I am. I'm gonna try to **slam-dunk** today.

8   What did you do last summer?

Useful Vocabulary

Try to use all of these words in your discussions today. Check them off as you use each one.

French kiss	키스	Peck on the cheek	뺨에 가볍게 키스하다
Awesome	멋진	Stuffed my face	포식하다
Weekend trip	주말여행	Concentrate on	집중하다
Fried an egg	계란후라이 했다	Text messages	문자메세지
Model student	모범생	Stuffed	배부른
Lightning fast	번개같이 빠른	Impatient	참을성 없는

Main Activity

Practise speaking using these questions using the correct grammar.

Ask more follow-up questions
(Who/When/Where/Why/What/Which/How…?)

Did you…?

- eat breakfast this morning?
- Yeah, I **stuffed my face** with rice and vegetables.

- travel overseas last summer?
- Yeah, I went on a **weekend trip** to Tokyo.

- have a part-time job last year?
- No, I wanted to fully **concentrate on** my studies.

- go to a nightclub (dance club) before you were 20?
- No, of course not. I was too busy studying because I'm a **model student.**

- cook something for yourself last week?
- Yes, I **fried an egg** last week. I was so proud of myself.

- kiss someone yesterday?
- Yeah, I gave my mom a **peck on the cheek**, but I didn't **French kiss** anyone.

More discussion questions…

(Be sure to ask follow-up questions, also.)

- **Was your dad** a fast runner when he was young?
- My dad tells me that he was **lightning fast**, but I don't believe him.

- What movie **did you see** recently? Did you like it?
- Yeah, I saw an **awesome** movie last week called '?'.

- **Did you have** breakfast/lunch/dinner before class?
- Yeah, I had a huge meal. Now I'm **stuffed.**

- Who was the last person that **you called** (on your phone)?
- I guess my mom was the last person I called on my phone. She doesn't like sending **text messages**.

- How long **did you wait** for the subway/bus this morning? Or did you drive or walk here?
- I had to wait about 10 minutes for my bus this morning. It was annoying because I'm **impatient.**

9 Take it easy!

Useful Vocabulary

 Try to use all of these words in your discussions today. Check them off as you use each one.

Sit up straight	똑바로 앉다	Please be kind	친절해라
Turn around and go back	돌아가라	Don't lie	거짓말 하지 마라
Talk to me	나한테 말하다	Look me in the eye	나를 봐
Work with me	나와 일해	Hang in there	거기 기다리고 있어
Stop complaining	불평하지마	Never give up	포기하지마
Tell me something interesting	뭔가 재미있는 이야기 해줘	Shut up	조용히해

Relax And Take it Easy!

 Imagine you are the military leader of your partner. **Order** them around for 1 minute. Now change roles.

▷ **Sit up straight.**

▷ **Look me in the eye.**

▷ **Work with me.**

▷ **Turn around and go back.**

▷ **Stop complaining.**

▷ **Talk to me.**

▷ **Tell me something interesting.**

▷ **Shut up.**

 You are now an extremely kind and wise life counsellor. Give good **advice** for a happy and healthy life. Take turns.

▷ **Please be kind.**

▷ **Don't lie.**

▷ **Hang in there.**

▷ **Never give up.**

Useful Vocabulary

 Try to use all of these words in your discussions today. Check them off as you use each one.

Punctual	시간을 지키는	Go on a diet	다이어트 시작하다
Ludicrous	우스꽝스러운	Conscientious	성실한
Put my feet up	쉬다	Considerate	배려하는
Dye my hair	염색하다	Overcrowded	초만원
Let her know	알리다	Hair salon	미장원
Sharp	정확히	Pouring	퍼붓는

Main Activity

Practise asking and answering these questions using the correct grammar.

**Ask more follow-up questions
(Who/When/Where/Why/What/Which/How…?)**

▷ **Are you going to study** or relax tonight?

▷ I've had a busy day, so I'm gonna just **put my feet up** tonight.

▷ Why **is/isn't your teacher gonna wear** a pink dress tomorrow?

▷ Because our teacher is a man, it would be a bit **ludicrous** if he wore a pink dress.

▷ How **are you going to be nicer** to your parents as you get older?

▷ I'm gonna try to be more and more **considerate** to my parents as I get older.

▷ **Are you gonna work harder** next class?

- I try to be as **conscientious** as possible in every class, of course.

- Where **are you gonna go swimming** when you go to Busan?

- I might just go to a local swimming pool to avoid the **overcrowded** Haeundae Beach.

More discussion questions...
(Be sure to ask follow-up questions, also.)

- **Are you ever gonna give up** (eating) chocolate?
- I only ever give up chocolate when I **go on a diet**.

- Where **are you gonna get** an ajumma perm when you're older?
- I'm gonna **dye my hair** at the same **hair salon** as my mom.

- When **is your friend gonna meet** you for lunch tomorrow?
- My friend's gonna meet me at 1pm **sharp**. She's always **punctual.**

- Why **are/aren't you gonna get** a taxi home after drinking tomorrow night?
- If it's **pouring** with rain, I might get a taxi home tomorrow night.

- Or **are you gonna stay out** all night? When **are**

- **you gonna call** your Mom to tell her you're not coming home?
- If I call my mom to **let her know**, I'm allowed to stay out all night.

II We're on vacation in 3 weeks

Useful Vocabulary

Try to use all of these words in your discussions today. Check them off as you use each one.

Drop by	잠시 들르다	Wander around	돌아다니다
My own apartment	내 소유 아파트	Play it by ear	되는데로
Dream partner	이상적인 파트너	Ancestral ceremony	제사
Free time	자유시간	Positive attitude	긍정적인 태도
Innovative	혁신적인	Efficiently	효율적으로
One-way trip	편도여행		

Main Activity

Practise asking and answering these questions using the correct grammar.

Ask more follow-up questions
(Who/When/Where/Why/What/Which/How...?)

- What are your immediate/short-term/long-term plans **after you graduate**?
- I think I might just take a **one-way trip** to Europe and see what happens.

- You said you have another class **at 5pm**, but what are you up to **later**?
- I'll probably **drop by** my friend's house and hang out.

- Do we have to prepare anything **for the next class**?
- We need to bring our textbook, a pen, and a **positive attitude.**

- Where do you think you'll live **in 10 years**?
- I'll hopefully live in **my own apartment.**

- What do you think you'll be doing **at 11pm** this Friday night?
- I haven't decided, yet. I'll just **play it by ear.**

- What do you usually do **on Friday nights in Summer**?
- I sometimes just **wander around** my neighborhood with my friends.

More discussion questions...
(Be sure to ask follow-up questions, also.)

- What do you think are the most important things to learn **during your time at university**?
- An important thing to learn is how to be **innovative**.

- Do you have to prepare anything **for Chuseok**?
- I should help to prepare some traditional food for the **ancestral ceremony.**

- What do you hope to achieve **by the end of this year**?
- I'd like to learn to study more **efficiently.**

- You will enjoy your life **until you get married**! Do you agree or disagree?
- I agree. I should enjoy my life as much as possible because I won't have much **free time** after getting married.

- Do you plan to get married **within the next 8 years**?
- Only if I find my **dream partner.**

12 Do ya wanna hang out on the weekend?

Useful Vocabulary

 Try to use all of these words in your discussions today. Check them off as you use each one.

Awkward	어색한	Luxurious	고급스러운
Reunion	동창회	Fancy	화려한
Hooked on	중독된	Stingy	구두쇠의
Essential	필수적인	Binge (drinking)	폭음하기
Kick back	쉬다	Get fit	건강해지다
Survive	살아남다	Pass out	술취하다
Black out	필름 끊기다		

Main Activity

Practise asking and answering these questions using the correct grammar.

**Ask more follow-up questions
(Who/When/Where/Why/What/Which/How…?)**

▷ Where is a great place to **kick back** on summer vacation?

▷ A **luxurious** tropical resort is a great place to **kick back** on summer vacation.

▷ Have you ever kept in touch with someone you've **broken up with**?

▷ No, not really. It's a bit **awkward** to keep in touch after breaking up.

▷ Do you usually have dinner at home or **eat out**?

▷ I have to be a bit **stingy** these days, so I usually try to have dinner at home.

▷ How often do you **get together** with your high school friends?

▷ Not that often, but we occasionally have a reunion.

▷ Do you think more people exercise outdoors or **work out** at a gym?

▷ I'm not exactly sure, but maybe more people try to **get fit** outdoors these days.

More discussion questions…

(Be sure to ask follow-up questions, also.)

▷ How hard do you think it is to **give up** smoking?

▷ I've been **hooked on** smoking for years, so it'll be really hard to give up.

▷ What are some things that you couldn't **do without**?

▷ I guess my phone is my most **essential** possession.

▷ What are you really **looking forward to** doing in the future?

▷ I'm really looking forward to staying in a **fancy** hotel one day.

▷ Do you know anyone who's **blacked out** or **passed out** from drinking too much?

▷ Yeah, after **binge drinking** I've seen people **pass out** and they probably also blacked out.

▷ How would you **get by on** W10,000 for a whole week?

▷ It would be difficult to **survive** for a whole week with only W10,000. Maybe I should just stay at home.

ENGLISH
FOR KOREANS

초판 1쇄 인쇄	2019년 1월 10일
초판 1쇄 발행	2019년 1월 15일

저 자	Greg Dawson
펴낸이	임 순 재
펴낸곳	**(주)한올출판사**
등 록	제11-403호
주 소	서울시 마포구 모래내로 83(성산동 한올빌딩 3층)
전 화	(02) 376-4298(대표)
팩 스	(02) 302-8073
홈페이지	www.hanol.co.kr
e-메 일	hanol@hanol.co.kr
ISBN	979-11-5685-735-8